SHORT WAL

Worcestershire
Pubs

Eleanor Smith

COUNTRYSIDE BOOKS
NEWBURY, BERKSHIRE

First Published 1995
© Eleanor Smith 1995

COUNTRYSIDE BOOKS
3 Catherine Road
Newbury, Berkshire

ISBN 1 85306 373 8

To Bob and Peggy

Designed by Mon Mohan
Cover illustration by Colin Doggett
Photographs by the author

Produced through MRM Associates Ltd., Reading
Typeset by The Midlands Book Typesetting Company, Loughborough
Printed by Woolnough Bookbinding, Irthlingborough

Contents

Area map showing locations of the walks.

Introduction

Worcestershire is one of England's smaller counties. Joined with Herefordshire in the reorganisation of local government in 1972/4, it has, nevertheless, kept its own identity. It is a flat area, bordered by the hills of the Malvern range to the west. The hills of Clent and Lickey form the northern boundary, while to the south are those of Dumbleton and Bredon. The rivers of Severn, Avon and Teme cross the county, creating pleasant lowland areas of watermeadows and the market gardening districts of which it is justly proud. Worcestershire is famed for its plums and apples, and in springtime a mist of blossom drifts across the acres of orchards.

Each of these 20 short walks is circular and is described in detail. The relevant OS Landranger map numbers and grid references are supplied. Public rights of way are used in all the routes, with the exception of canal towpaths, which are permissive paths for walkers. A nearby place of interest is incorporated in the walk or referred to at the end, the abbeys of Pershore and Evesham, for example, and some fine churches. This is Elgar's county and is where much of his stirring, passionate music was composed. His birthplace, now a museum of his works, is also included in a walk.

The Malvern Hills present a challenge which I have not quite taken up. By using the lower slopes, however, one can enjoy the pleasures of hill walking without the pressures. Gentle routes near the distinctive Abberley Hill and the open spaces of the country parks of both Lickey and Clent have also been included. Bredon Hill, with a summit rising to 960 ft, presides over, and shelters, the Vale of Evesham. Again I have used the lower slopes. Not so with Broadway. The tower, a landmark for miles around, seems to draw one to the very top of this northern escarpment of the Cotswolds.

The river valleys play their part in creating a landscape popular with holidaymakers and boating enthusiasts. They also make an ideal place to walk with ever-changing scenery and no hills . . .

A word of advice – good, firm boots or shoes are necessary even on these short walks. A sudden storm, unmown grass, a slippery slope may all be hazards without protective footwear.

As for the pubs, landlords are becoming increasingly aware that family hostelries are very much a place of the future. Gone, or perhaps going, are the days of a 'pint and a pie'. Imaginative meals for all ages, smaller portions for children and, in some cases, for senior citizens, are certainly offered at many pubs. Not all those I have chosen have family rooms but each will welcome family groups and create an atmosphere where younger members of the party are made to feel at home. Some have room for indoor play while more have an outside activity area.

Times of opening have been noted. Parking permission has been agreed but it is, perhaps, advisable to check this before setting off for your walk, especially if you are eating afterwards.

Happy rambling along the paths and tracks of this lovely county. Enjoy the peaceful waterways and the windswept common land. When you have sampled some of these pub walks around Worcestershire you will assuredly agree with me that the only way to see a county is to walk it.

Eleanor Smith
Spring 1995

Publisher's Note

We hope that you obtain considerable enjoyment from this book; great care has been taken in its preparation. However, changes of landlord and actual closures are sadly not uncommon. Likewise, although at the time of publication all routes followed public rights of way or permitted paths, diversion orders can be made and permissions withdrawn.

We cannot of course be held responsible for such diversion orders and any resultant inaccuracies in the text which result from these or any other changes to the routes nor any damage which might result from walkers trespassing on private property. We are anxious that all details covering the walks and the pubs are kept up to date and would therefore welcome information from readers which would be relevant to future editions.

1 Bewdley
The Little Pack Horse

Bewdley has a long history of river trading. Originally known as Beaulie, beautiful place, it is, indeed, well named. Life centred around the river Severn, the life-line for trade and industry until the coming of more direct transport links. Riverside meadows have now been made into pleasure grounds, boats move along the swiftly flowing water and the natural river life passes its time as it always did. The town has a church on an island in its centre, a bustling Saturday market and a main street where it is scarcely possible for two cars to pass – and I shall be surprised if you manage to leave without some purchase from one of the intriguing antique or curio shops.

It is here, in the High Street, that the Little Pack Horse is located, a truly traditional inn with ancient black beams and flagstone floors. Old photographs decorate the walls and the mosaic mural on the passage wall is truly a masterpiece. This is Bewdley's oldest pub, known to have been a hostelry since 1608, with some parts of the building dating to 1584. It is in what was the business end of the town, where warehouses and grain stores once conducted their numerous transactions. Most have now become houses and apartments but the character still remains. I am told that, at one time, there were more pubs per head of population here than anywhere else in the country. It seems to me that there are still quite a few ...

Children are welcome at the Little Pack Horse, families being accommodated in a converted stable block. The main room of the pub has a bar set on sleepers from the Severn Valley Railway, while the uprights are barrels. A superb elm counter top is graced with shining brass plaques. Lunchtimes are deservedly busy. Who would not enjoy one of the following – the 'Famous Desperate Dan Pie', succulent steak and kidney cooked in Guinness, a king-size Cradley pork sausage or some fresh home-baked ham with parsley sauce? A Pack Horse sandwich and coffee can also be a meal in itself. Smaller portions for smaller people are served, too. Now for the beers. Four traditional ales are on tap at any one time. Ruddles County bitter, Marston's Pedigree or their own Lumphammer bitter, which is as potent as it sounds, are just three of them. Wines and lagers, ciders and spirits, the choice is yours. The opening times are 11 am to 3 pm and 7 pm to 11 pm (all day on Saturdays in peak season), with the usual Sunday times. Food is available from 12 noon to 2 pm, and in the evening from 6 pm to 9.30 pm (summer) or 6.30 pm to 9 pm (winter). A friendly welcome, cheerful conversation, history all around you and some more in the making – this is a place to remember.

Telephone: 01299 403762.

How to get there: Bewdley lies on the B4190, south-west of Kidderminster. On reaching the town make for the church on the island in the centre. Turn left, along High Street, very narrow, but two-way traffic. The pub is about 1/4 mile along this street on the left.

Parking: There is no parking space at the pub so turn immediately left on reaching it and continue to a public car park on your right.

Length of the walk: 2 1/2 miles. Map: OS Landranger 138 Kidderminster and Wyre Forest area (inn GR 787751).

This walk takes you along the river Severn, through the Blackstone Meadows Country Park, past Ribbesford church and on part of the Worcestershire Way. You will also pass the sites of the old Snuff

Mill and the Palace of Tickenhill. A pleasant country walk with ever-changing scenery. Well signed and easily walked.

The Walk

Leaving the Pack Horse inn, turn left and then left again down Lax Lane. Notice the old boys' school on the right as you make your way down towards the river. One of the original fords across the Severn was located at the bottom of this street. On reaching the river turn right and follow the footpath downstream, marked 'Footpath 64'. When you reach the bypass bridge you will pick up the Worcestershire Way. Proceed under the bridge and continue on the riverside footpath, signed 'Footpath 12R'.

After leaving the bridge you pass through Blackstone Meadows Country Park, created by Hereford and Worcester County Countryside Services. You should be able to see the caves in the red sandstone at the base of Blackstone Rock across the river from this point. The picnic table area is well mown and a pleasant place to rest awhile. Keep to the left as you walk through this part and take the river path again.

On reaching the road turn left. Cross over, carefully, and walk for about 50 yards towards a lane leading off on the right, signed 'Ribbesford Church', a bridleway. As you walk up the lane look to your left where you will see Ribbesford Manor with its twin domes reaching towards the sky. This is where Free French officers were trained during the Second World War, and General de Gaulle spent some time here. Take a look at the church and rejoin the path, following the 'Worcestershire Way north' signs. Keep on the wide cinder track and notice the lovely old barn opposite the church. Bear left and continue through the tunnel, passing under the Bewdley bypass. Ignore the left turn here and keep straight on, still on the wide track.

On reaching a road, cross over and go through a kissing gate, still on the Worcestershire Way. The sign on the gate says 'Snuff Mill Fishing Pool'. When you reach the entrance to the pools, with the gate on your left, walk on for a few yards to where there is a stile on your left. Go over this and onto an enclosed path. About halfway along this path, where there is a break in the dam, look to your left. Across the field, close to some trees, is the site of the old snuff mill which gives this area its name. Continue along the path to the wood and go over a stile. Cross the bridge and then go over another stile.

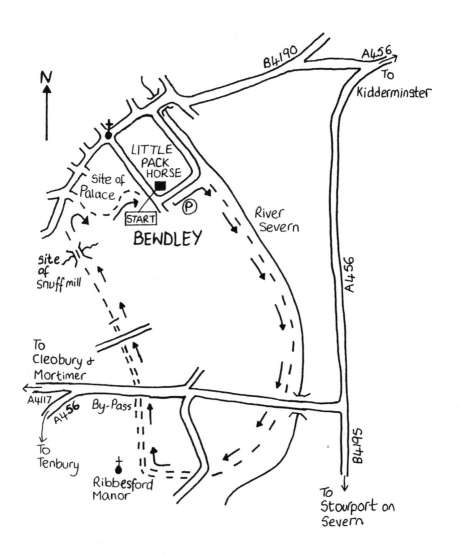

N

B4190

A456
To
Kidderminster

LITTLE PACK HORSE

Site of Palace

Ⓟ

START

BEWDLEY

River Severn

site of snuff mill

A456

To Cleobury & Mortimer

A4117

A456

By-Pass

To Tenbury

Ribbesford Manor

B4195

To Stourport on Severn

This bridge crosses the Snuff Mill brook, which runs under Lax Lane to the river Severn.

On reaching Snuff Mill Lane turn right. At the end of the lane turn sharp right, joining 'Footpath 60' leading up to Tickenhill house. This is the site of the old palace where Prince Arthur, the eldest son of Henry VII, held court as Lord President of the Marches. Later, in 1525, Henry VIII sent his young daughter, Princess Mary (subsequently Queen Mary), to live here.

Near the top of the drive there is a gate and stile on your right. Cross over this stile and take the footpath, bearing left and keeping close to the hedge. There are views from here across to Bewdley and the safari park. You should also be able to see the top of the Clent Hills. Pass through a gap in the hedge and turn right, marked 'Footpath 62'. Continue on this path until you reach a row of houses with beautiful gardens. At the junction turn left and follow the lane to the High Street. Cross carefully to the pub.

Places of interest nearby

The *West Midland Safari Park* is close by, well signed from Bewdley, and offers many species of animals, in very pleasant surroundings.

The *Severn Valley Steam Railway*, Kidderminster to Bridgnorth, passes through the town and can be joined at the station, also well signed.

2 Hartlebury
The White Hart

Hartlebury is a village surrounding a castle. Attractive cottages, tree-lined drives and an interesting church all contribute to the charm. Home of the Bishops of Worcester, the castle's fortifications were begun when Simon de Montfort was leading the barons against the King. During the Civil War it was used for captive royalists. The church contains many treasures, which include an ancient episcopal throne and a partly Norman font decorated with flowers and diamonds.

The White Hart, a large, picturesque pub, lies in the centre of the village. Decorated with hanging baskets and ablaze with colour during the summer months, it retains its old world atmosphere amid comfortable and spacious surroundings. An L-shaped lounge bar, leading out to the attractive beer garden, is well furnished and has plenty of room for sitting down with a meal. Children are welcome in the eating areas and should find sufficient space outside to be able to burn off some of their energy. A play area, safely fenced, is located adjoining the car park.

A wide-ranging bar menu offers such choices as rump steak baguette, a long crusty roll with steak and garnish. The 'Harvester', which includes mature Cheddar and boiled ham served with a white or brown cottage roll, is another favourite. Omelettes with various fillings are especially good. A 'specials' blackboard is a feature of the house. Good food and good value seem to be the watchwords for this pub and a busy lunchtime trade shows the esteem in which it is held. A separate evening menu provides an even wider choice. The delights of lemon brûlée and banoffi cream pie are just two of the very tempting sweets available at both mealtimes. Children's portions are popular with the the youngsters. The White Hart is an M&B house. Traditional Brew XI, Banks's Mild and Bass are all on draught. Lagers include both Tennent's Extra and Low Alcohol, along with Carling Black Label. Three ciders are on offer, strong and medium Cider Master, sweet Autumn Gold and Dry Blackthorn. The pub is open from 11 am to 3 pm and 6 pm to 11 pm on Monday to Saturday, and from 12 noon to 3 pm and 7 pm to 10.30 pm on Sunday. Food is served during all opening times, except on Sundays.

Telephone: 01299 250286.

How to get there: From the Stourport on Severn bypass, south of Kidderminster, take the B4193 Hartlebury road. On entering the village, just past the castle/museum entrance, you will see the pub on your left.

Parking: There is ample parking at the pub.

Length of the walk: 3 miles. Map: OS Landranger 138 Kidderminster and Wyre Forest area (inn GR 838708).

Hartlebury Common is in the care of the Countryside Commission. The walk takes you onto this natural heathland, through a leafy, damp wood and skirting some old ponds. A wealth of wildlife attracts the eye as bullrushes stand guard around the pools. We spotted a jay, beautiful and solitary, yellow-hammers and larks. Coots and mallards, perhaps with their families strung out behind them, seem to enjoy the frenzied activity as they dash among the reeds and rushes. A plantation of pines and the seasonal variations, of the shimmering yellow gorse and the lovely blue haze of bluebells in the woodland area, contribute to a fascinating year-round walk.

The Walk

Leave the pub car park and walk down the road towards the castle entrance. Keep on the pavement for about 400 yards until reaching a lake on your right. This is part of the old castle moat. Cross carefully here and walk into Hilditch Lane. Continue along this quiet, leafy lane for about 200 yards to where you will see a sign on your right, placed there by the Countryside Commission, leading into a wood.

A well-used path leads through the mixed woodland, with a stream on your right. Ignore a flight of wooden-faced steps on your right and continue straight ahead until reaching a lane. Turn right over the pool outflow and right again at another sign. Walk beside the pool for a few yards. Take the first left fork up into a wood and follow the path through the trees, bearing slightly left, uphill. On reaching a lane and car park, notice the area of blown sand, quite deep in places, and cross the car park towards the left-hand corner. Walk up the wide track, following the blue marker. Keep on this track, bearing to the right towards a plantation of pine trees. The path passes between two small plantations. Keep straight on the main track and you will arrive at Wilden Top car park and picnic area. There are views from here across to Stourport and the Severn valley.

The return journey begins from the left-hand corner of the car park, turning back onto the common. Take this path, which will join the main track you used on the outgoing route. Just before reaching the plantation of pine trees, take a left-hand path and keep on this until reaching a cross-path junction. Turn left. You are now back on the track to the bottom car park.

Cross the lane and follow the track through the woods again. However, on reaching the pond, turn left towards an iron gate. There is a gap here. Walk through it and on to a path skirting the pond. This is where the bullrushes stand proud and waterlilies float in their clusters.

Continue to walk alongside the pond and bear right between two pools. This will take you to the wooden-faced steps noticed on the outward walk. Climb these and turn left. Now follow the path

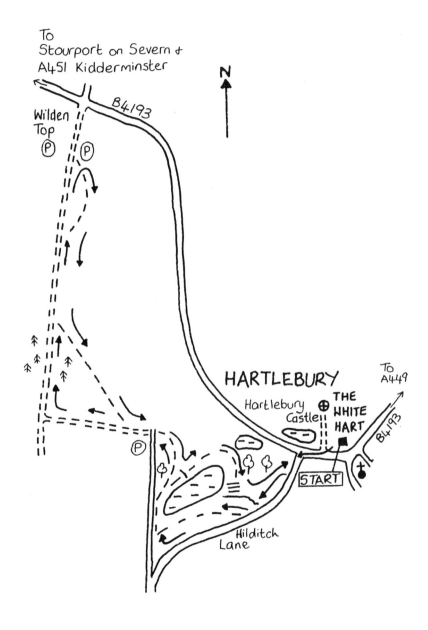

To
Stourport on Severn &
A451 Kidderminster

B4193

Wilden
Top
Ⓟ   Ⓟ

N

HARTLEBURY

To
A449

Hartlebury
Castle

THE
WHITE
HART

B4193

Ⓟ

START

Hilditch
Lane

Village house at Hartlebury.

back to the lane, turn left and so return to the main road and the pub.

Places of interest nearby

The *Castle* at Hartlebury is divided into three. The southern end, adjoining the chapel, is the residence of the present Bishop. The central block houses state rooms and the beautiful library, and the north wing is now the *Worcestershire County Museum*. The museum is open daily (except on Saturdays and Good Friday), from 10 am to 5 pm on Monday to Thursday, and from 2 pm to 5 pm on Friday and Sunday. A beautiful avenue of lime trees leads from the road to the castle entrance.

③ Great Witley
The Hundred House Hotel

The Hundred House Hotel is set in rolling countryside in an exceptionally beautiful part of Worcestershire. The wooded Abberley Hill rises to the rear of the hotel and the Woodbury Hills to the front. The name is unusual and originates from the days when the oldest part of the building was used as a collecting house for the tithes gathered from 100 districts of the county. A welcoming atmosphere greets you as you enter the spacious lounges, which are a feature of this hotel. While catering for weddings and other functions, this popular place also looks after the passing traveller and walker.

A good selection of tasty bar meals are served, while a formal restaurant is available for those wishing to take a full meal. There is also a traditional Sunday lunch. Home-made beef pie or a sea food platter, a ploughman's lunch or a prawn open sandwich are just a few of the items on the bar menu. Vegetarian dishes include fruit and vegetable chilli served with rice. The children should be happy with the usual favourites, which are served in generous portions. There is not a family room as such but there is space for children away from the bars, and a garden area for summer days. A well-kept cellar offers Banks's traditional ales, Bass and a guest beer. Draught Guinness, Bulmer's Original and Strongbow ciders are also available. A comprehensive wine list, lagers and spirits, including a good selection of malt whiskies, should please most tastes. The pub is open on Monday to Saturday from 11 am to 3 pm and 7 pm to 11 pm, with the usual Sunday hours. Bar meals are served from 12 noon to 2 pm and 7 pm to 9.45 pm every day except Sunday, when they are available just in the evening, from 7 pm to 9 pm.

Telephone: 01299 896888.

How to get there: Set at the junction of the A443 Droitwich and Worcester road, the A451 Stourport and Kidderminster road and the B4203 Bromyard road, this hotel is easily accessible from most major centres of the county.

Parking: There is a large car park at the hotel.

Length of the walk: 3½ miles. Map: OS Landranger 138 Kidderminster and Wyre Forest area (inn GR 751663).

Avoiding the steep climb of Abberley Hill, the walk incorporates field and woodland paths, some high enough to give splendid views across the surrounding countryside. You will pass close to the Gothic clock tower rising above the trees in the grounds of Abberley Hall school. Part of the Worcestershire Way has been used. You will also pass through the village of Abberley, a good halfway mark, where a visit can be made to the Norman church.

The Walk

Leave the car park and walk in front of the hotel along the footpath beside the A443 towards Tenbury. Just after the junction with the B4203, the Bromyard road, cross carefully, to take a signed track on the left (the sign is on your right). Walk up this track, through a gate and uphill, passing a pond on your right. You will soon reach the Abberley Hall school buildings. Turn right as you join the Worcestershire Way. The clock tower will be on your right. There is, unfortunately, no access to this interesting building. A deer farm on your left may well encourage you to stop and admire these gentle creatures.

18

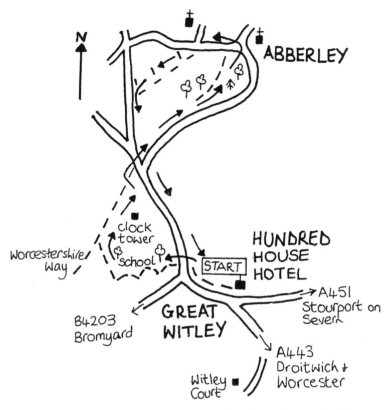

Continue on the path until you reach the main road. Cross over
carefully to the lane opposite. Walk up this rather steep hill, passing
various footpath signs en route. Where the Worcestershire Way
goes off to the right, almost at the top of the hill, keep straight
on for about another 200 yards until you reach a sign on your
left, waymarked with a 'circular loop'. Take this path leading into
woods and descending rather steeply between the trees. Cross over
a stile and keep left in the adjacent field, making for a stile
ahead. Over this, cross the driveway to another stile and walk
across the next field, making for the bottom left-hand corner.
Climb the stile here and turn right as you join a track. Go
down this track, passing some houses as you enter the village of
Abberley.

This is an interesting village with large houses, a pub and a

Witley Court, Great Witley.

Norman church, clustered together to form the village centre. Turn left, walk a few yards and turn left again at the T-junction. In about 250 yards look for a footpath sign on your left pointing across a field. Go through the gate and, keeping to the bottom of the two fields, walk straight ahead to a gate leading onto a lane and the new part of Abberley. Turn left and cross over onto the pavement. Continue along this lane until you reach the main road.

You now have a choice of return routes from here to the pub. Either use the same route by which you began the walk, through the school grounds, or turn left and walk the footpath alongside the road, back to the pub.

Places of interest nearby

Witley Court lies about 2 miles away from the hotel. It is well signed off the A443 road towards Worcester. This vast shell of a building is one of the most spectacular country house ruins in England.

4 Holt Fleet
The Wharf Inn

The Wharf Inn takes its name from the coal wharf which was located there from the mid 19th century until the 1920s. The river Severn, beside which it is situated, played an important part in the movement of all commodities until railways and roads began to show a faster and more direct route to the industrial centres of the country. The nearby Holt Bridge, built in 1828, is the last one over the Severn before reaching Worcester. It commands a splendid view up the river. The coal wharf of yesterday has become a busy, thriving pub, catering for fishermen, boating enthusiasts and those people who just like being by the river.

This is no small, local inn but a large, bustling place with a holiday visitor trade from the nearby caravans and chalets. There is ample space for the children, including a good-sized family room overlooking the river. An outdoor playground with slides and climbing frames can keep the youngsters happily occupied while parents watch from the conveniently placed garden tables and chairs. Food is geared to the fast food outlet it is. Hot, tasty soups, salads, sandwiches and generously portioned basket meals are some of the favourites. A hot beef roll or a chilli served with rice and salad are others. Sunday roasts are a feature. Vegetarian meals are also available. The children's menu includes all the usual favourites. For the very young it offers sweets such as jelly and ice-cream or a sponge pudding. The pub is a Whitbread house and serves Whitbread and Banks's draught beers. Strongbow and Woodpecker cider are on offer, as are Murphy's stout and Stella Artois and Heineken lagers. The opening times are 12 noon to 3 pm and 7 pm to 11 pm every day, with extended hours during the summer months, depending on the weather conditions.

Telephone: 01905 620289.

How to get there: Holt Fleet is approximately 6 miles from Worcester, in a north-westerly direction. Take the A443 from Worcester, signed 'Tenbury', which passes through Hallow. After about 5 miles look for a sign for Droitwich and Kidderminster. Turn right here along a road to join the A4133, Droitwich road. Turn right and continue for about 1 mile until you cross a bridge over the river Severn. Look for the 'Wharf Inn' sign on your right and an approach track to it.

Parking: There is plenty of parking space at the pub.

Length of the walk: 2 miles. Map: OS Landranger 150 Worcester, The Malverns and surrounding area (inn GR 826632).

Holt Fleet is a place of great charm, busy with river craft, in the summertime, passing through the adjacent lock. A pleasant, easy stroll will take you alongside this and so into the watermeadows beyond. Riverside chalets, fishermen quietly watching their bobbing floats and the ever-present wildlife of the river all contribute to a relaxing walk.

The Walk

From the pub take the riverside path towards the bridge. Go under it, continue to follow the river through the small parking area and pass between two white posts onto a tarmac road. You will now see Holt Lock. Pass the lock and adjacent cottage and go through a gate onto a grassy riverside pathway. Holiday bungalows

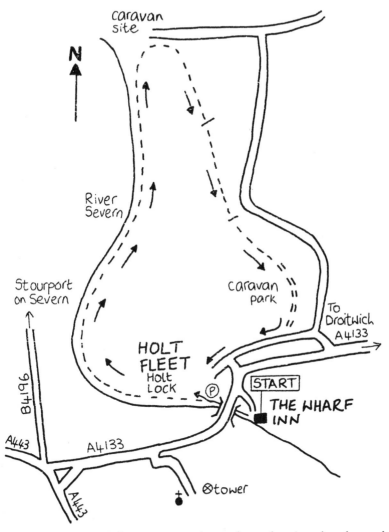

are now on your right. Keep on the path as the river bends to the right.

A peaceful place this. The bungalows are left behind and the river takes on a shady, slow pace as it meanders between the trees. A small settlement of caravans and chalets comes into sight on the other side

Holt Lock.

of the river. As you approach a stile leading into a holiday site, do not go over it, but turn right and follow the hedge towards a stile in the top right corner of the field. Do not go over this either. Turn right and walk back, keeping close to the embankment on your left. Still alongside the embankment, climb a stile. On reaching a small holiday chalet on your left look for another stile ahead. Go over this, through the field and enter a caravan park.

The right of way bears left between the caravans and then bears right. Walk along a few yards to the next left turn into another caravan area. Turn into this and walk along a made-up track until reaching a junction. Take the right-hand track here and continue along it until reaching a crossroads. Turn right. This lane will lead you back to the bridge. Retrace your steps from here to the pub and car park.

Places of interest nearby

You may like to take a look at *Holt church* and *castle* after your walk. Drive over the bridge and take the first left-hand turn. Continue along this road until you reach the church and tower opposite to each other.

Lulsley
The Fox and Hounds

The Fox and Hounds, close to Knightwick and quickly reached from Worcester, has all the features of an ideal country pub, including good food, well-kept beers and a comfortable and welcoming atmosphere. Situated off the beaten track, it has spacious gardens ablaze with flowers in the summer, which set off to perfection the large Victorian building. It takes its name from the original Fox and Hounds which was situated about $1/2$ mile up the road. The lounge and dining room have pleasant views across the countryside and a patio seating area makes a splendid place in which to sit and enjoy a drink and snack on warm days. Children are welcome in this pub, with a good area away from the bar for them to sit. Horses kept in the field adjoining the garden are an added attraction.

There is a wide and tempting choice of dishes. The lunch menu offers such snacks as home-cooked gammon sandwich on granary bread or a smoked turkey ploughman's. Pies and casseroles include Hunter's Chicken, lamb rosemary or beef in Guinness. The popular Hungry Hounds mixed grill is all that a grill should be. A blackboard

menu adds to the variety, all of which can be complemented by Worthington or Bass real ale. A good variety of malt whiskies and a selection of white, red and sparkling wines are also offered. The opening times are 12 noon to 3 pm and 6 pm to 11 pm on Monday to Saturday, with the usual Sunday hours.
Telephone: 01886 821228.

How to get there: Leave Worcester by the A4103. As the road takes a sharp left turn at a hotel and filling station, turn right, signed 'Leigh'. Continue through Alfrick towards Knightwick. You will come to the Fox and Hounds on your right just past the nature reserve.

Parking: The pub has a large car park.

Length of the walk: 3½ miles. Map: OS Landranger 150 Worcester, The Malverns and surrounding area (inn GR 739547).

The walk starts with a climb up to Ravenshill Wood, offering splendid views, and continues, on footpaths, part of the Worcestershire Way and a lane, to the attractive village of Alfrick. On the return route there is an opportunity to visit the Ravenshill Woodland Reserve.

The Walk
Turn left on leaving the pub for about 10 yards, to where you see a footpath sign on your right. Follow this sign up the farm drive. At a fork keep on the tarmac drive, bearing left. Notice the breeding pens for pheasants here. On reaching the farm entrance gates turn left, following the waymarks through a gate. Continue to follow the signs in front of the house, then pass a barn to the next waymark and a stile. Look back from here to the Malvern Hills. Still keeping to the fence on your right, walk towards the wood, to where you see the Worcestershire Way sign going to the right. Turn left but do not go over the stile into the wood. Instead keep along the top of the field, with the wood on your right, until you reach the double gates. Through these there are more Worcestershire Way signs. Turn left, following the signs. You have now climbed sufficiently high to be able to enjoy some spectacular views over Herefordshire.

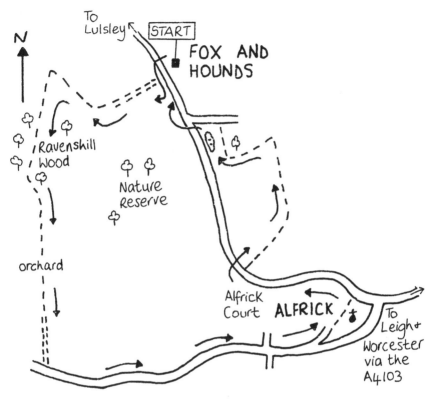

Keep to the well-defined footpath, appreciating even wider views here as you turn a corner. Continue straight ahead, ignoring the gate on your right. You will now pass by an orchard, a cloud of blossom in the spring and aglow with apples in the late summer. On reaching a driveway turn right. Walk down to a lane. Turn left.

The lane goes downhill for a while and then uphill to a fork. Keep straight on. Notice a gazebo in the cottage garden here. Ignore the right turn and continue downhill for about ¼ mile into Alfrick village. There are many interesting houses, some from oast house conversions. Go straight over the crossroads and turn first left, signed 'footpath to St Mary's church'. Walk through a small estate of retirement bungalows into the churchyard. Pause a while to look at the church. It contains a Jacobean pulpit, while the lower part of the chancel screen is composed of pieces of Tudor carving.

The cruck barn at Leigh.

On leaving the churchyard through the main entrance gate, turn left and walk on until you reach a crossroads, with the post office on your right. Turn left here, following the 'Lulsley' sign. Bear right as you reach Alfrick Court. Continue on the lane to two cottages on your right. Immediately past them is a gateway. At this point it is possible to continue on the lane to arrive at the same point, Ravenshill Reserve, as you will when using the footpath.

Turn right through the gateway, keeping to the right-hand hedge. Make for a water tank. There is a three-way sign here. Turn left in front of the water tank, then right. If the field is cropped there should be a walkway through it. However, you may have to walk round the field, making for the coppice on your right, ahead. The path actually goes through the coppice but it can be overgrown in high summer. I walked round it. On reaching the stile out of the coppice, follow the waymark towards a wood ahead. There is a good path between the fields. On reaching the wood turn left. It is rather difficult to see the waymark and the path seems to encourage you to go right – don't.

Continue along this path for about 200 yards and look for a gap in the hedge – no waymark that I could see. You need to search hard for the gap, particularly in the summer. In about 4 yards you will come to a stile. Go over this and turn right, following a defined footpath.

Before following the path, just walk a few yards ahead, to where you can climb up to look down on to Lulsley Lagoon – a lovely spot with herons, geese and other wildfowl. The path goes over a small bridge and makes towards a gate in the hedgerow straight ahead. At the lane turn left and, almost immediately, right.

If you wish to include a visit to the nature reserve, turn left here for a few yards. You will see the reserve on your right.

Walk along the lane and, in about 400 yards, you will arrive back at the pub.

Places of interest nearby

Ravenshill Woodland Reserve is close to the pub and can be included in the walk. A natural history exhibition in the Discovery Centre, while quite small, is very interesting. It is open from 1st March to 31st October.

Leigh, on the road between Worcester and Alfrick, has a particularly fine *cruck barn*, adjacent to the church.

6 Upper Broadheath
The Plough

Known to have been an inn for over 100 years, this pub has been sympathetically modernised to become the popular place it is today. Very close to Elgar's birthplace and on the Elgar Trail, the village attracts many visitors who are tracing the traditions of the famous Worcestershire composer. Welcoming staff and a comfortable lounge and dining area make this a pleasant place to be for a meal and a drink. A children's play area outside with swings and slides also has chairs and tables to take advantage of the sunny days.

Senior citizens are considered here, with a 'less quantity – less price' policy. Children also have their own menu. Roast duck suppers on Thursdays, fresh fish on Wednesdays and a self service salad bar at all times are just part of what is on offer. A local 'Elgar' cheese is featured with the ploughman's lunches and a satisfying baguette can be made up on request. A well-stocked bar offers a range of cask ales. Theakston Best Bitter, Murphy's stout and a choice of lagers are included. Strongbow and Woodpecker ciders are a popular local drink. The opening times are 12 noon to 2 pm and 6 pm to 11 pm on Monday to Saturday, with the usual Sunday hours. Food is served from 12 noon to 2 pm and 6 pm to 9.30 pm.

Telephone: 01905 333677.

How to get there: From Worcester, take the A44 Leominster road. In about 4 miles look for a sign to the right for 'Broadheath' and 'Elgar's Birthplace'. About 2 miles down this road you will see the pub on your right.

Parking: There is a large car park at the pub.

Length of the walk: 2 miles. Map: OS Landranger 150 Worcester, The Malverns and surrounding area (inn GR 806558).

This is a relatively short walk exploring the field paths around the village of Upper Broadheath. Birthplace of Elgar, the museum is on the route and offers a glimpse of the life and works of this famous man. The home of Elgar's sister and a moated farmhouse are also en route and should you be walking this way during early autumn you will probably see a field full of the fungi known as puff balls.

The Walk

From the pub turn left. Walk for about 200 yards, passing the museum on your left. Look for a stile in the hedge, with a footpath sign on your right. Climb the stile. There are views of the Malvern Hills from here. Keeping the hedge on your right, walk to the next stile, skirting a stretch of woodland. Over the stile and still keeping the same direction, make for a hedge and stile leading onto the A44. There is a wide grass verge here so traffic should be no problem. Turn right. Walk for about 100 yards to where you see a gate, no waymark sign, on your right.

If you walk about another 100 yards up the road you come to an interesting garden centre and coffee shop. Afterwards, retrace your steps to the gate.

Climb the fence next to the gate and go diagonally left towards the top left-hand corner of the field. There is a gate here which you walk

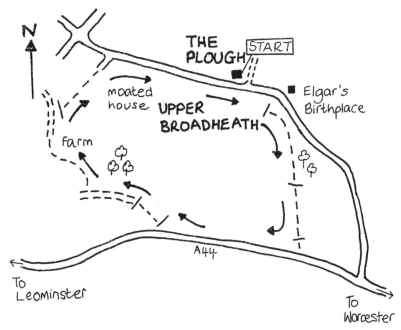

through into a wide, enclosed track. Continue along the track where, just before reaching a wood on your right, is a field where puff balls may be found, in season. The wood behind is a mass of bluebells in the spring and is a haunt of badgers. The black and white house to the right was the home of Elgar's sister.

The track bears to the left but you need to walk straight ahead, making for the farmhouse of Upper Lighwood Farm. The path goes between the house and buildings and bears right along a track. Just past the front entrance to the farmhouse, which is a lovely old house with well-kept gardens, you will see a stile, waymarked, on your right. Go over this into the field and keep to the footpath which goes round the edge of the field, with the hedge on your right. On reaching a driveway, the entrance to Newbury Farm, which was a moated farmhouse, turn left. There is some evidence of the moat still to be seen, rather overgrown, just on your right.

There is a magnificent granary barn, also on your right, as you walk along the drive. As you approach the road some Scots pine trees

Elgar's Birthplace.

tower majestically above the low hedges, proving themselves worthy of the mention made of them by Elgar in a letter to his friend, Alice Stuart Wortley, in 1920.

Turn right and the pub will be on your left.

Places of interest nearby

Elgar's birthplace and *museum* of his works, open daily, except Wednesday, from 10.30 am to 6 pm (in the summer) or 1.30 pm to 4.30 pm (in the winter).

The village is very close to Worcester, where the *cathedral*, *Guildhall* and *pottery* are all of special interest.

Wynds Point
The Malvern Hills Hotel

Standing beside one of the main roads across the Malvern Hills, this 16th century building has been a hostelry for all that time. Called the British Camp Hotel for many years, it was named after one of the most recognisable landmarks on the Malvern Hills – the Herefordshire Beacon or British Camp, as it is also known, from the Iron Age fort on its summit, which is thought to be of Celtic origin. Just inside Worcestershire, the county boundary sign of Herefordshire being across the road, the hotel is the ideal place to quench your thirst or satisfy the pangs of hunger either before or after your walk. It is a friendly place, with spacious, comfortably furnished bars and lounges, and outdoor tables and chairs for the warmer days. Overnight accommodation is also available.

Children are made welcome in the 'Peter Pocket' room. Who was Peter Pocket? A renowned highwayman, we are told, with infamous exploits renowned for miles around. Today 'his' room is a pleasant place to enjoy your meal and drink. Children over twelve are allowed to eat in the bars and dogs may accompany their owners. Four well-kept ales are always on draught, Bass, Hook Norton, Wood

and Hobsons. The lagers include Stella Artois and Carling Black Label. A wine list to suit most tastes and the usual range of spirits are also on offer. A blackboard menu which changes daily offers a variety of dishes. Home-made soup, ploughman's lunch and jacket potatoes are always there. The hot 'dish of the day' varies, chicken, pork and prawn risotto being an example. A vegetable and pasta bake or a Spanish omelette should suit the vegetarian. Home-made sweets are served in generous portions. The pub is open from 10.30 am to 2.30 pm and 6 pm to 11 pm on Monday to Saturday, and from 12 noon to 3 pm and 7 pm to 10.30 pm on Sunday. Lunchtime food is served from 12 noon to 2 pm seven days a week and in the evenings from 7 pm to 10 pm (9 pm on Sunday).
Telephone: 01684 540237 and 540690.

How to get there: Wynds Point lies south of Great Malvern, on the A449 Worcester to Ross-on-Wye road. From Worcester the road passes through Malvern Wells and skirts the hills until, after a fairly steep climb, it reaches the hotel on the right, facing British Camp and a large car park.

Parking: There is limited parking at the pub. A public car park is just opposite.

Length of the walk: 4 miles. Map: OS Landranger 150 Worcester, The Malverns and surrounding area (inn GR 765405).

This is a Malvern Hills route on which you can enjoy the magnificent scenery without having to climb to great heights to do so. The path from Wynds Point, close to British Camp, takes in the Wyche Cutting, where one can see some of the oldest rocks in the world. Splendid views over both Worcestershire and Herefordshire, the Severn valley and the distant Black Mountains are a reward for the gentle inclines which have to be included. Choose a day of clear skies and enjoy this pleasant walk along old tracks and paths. Pass through woodland and open heath where, in summer, the harebells blow gently in the breeze.

The Walk
From the pub car park turn right off the A449 onto the B4232, Jubilee Drive, passing toilets on your left. Keep on the right-hand side of the

road along a path which bears right through some trees, into a car park area. Make for the top car park and take the track leading to the right, uphill. As you reach a bench on your left, take the right fork instead of climbing over the hill in front of you. At the next junction of paths take the right fork. There is a wonderful viewpoint here for views across the Severn valley towards Upton. St Wulstan's church lies below, the burial place of Sir Edward Elgar.

The path now wends its way round until it reaches Berington's Quarry, where the oldest Malvernian rocks are exposed. The granite is interveined with red pegmatite on the right and white quartz on the left.

At the next fork and bench keep to the left. Staying on the left-hand trail at the next fork, continue winding gently uphill through woodland until you reach another junction of paths. Take the left one.

This area of woodland is pleasantly sheltered, whether it be from wind or sun. While blocking the views, it makes a change from the exposed heath of the higher slopes. Keep straight on at the next fork. You are now entering open country used for sheep pasture, although, nowadays, sheep are few and far between. Worrying by unrestrained dogs has caused the farmers to remove their flocks. The Malvern Hills Conservators are now responsible for checking the tree seedlings, once grazed off by the sheep.

At the next bench keep left. As you reach the main track turn right. You are now on high, open heath, where the harebells flutter in summer and the views are quite magnificent on both sides. To avoid climbing to the top of the hill, take the left-hand path. As you join the main track again, Malvern Wells lies below and the Worcestershire Beacon ahead.

Bear right to reach the road and then left to walk through the Wyche Cutting. It is a busy road but there is a good footpath. One can appreciate the immense rock hewing operation that had to take place to make a road through this granite. Wyche is derived from the Old English word for salt and the cutting is believed to be named from the ancient packhorse 'saltway' which crossed the hills here. It dates from 1836, being widened in 1840 and again at the turn of the century. A valuable find was made in this area when materials were dug out for road building, from a steep valley above the new road, and two hoards of currency bars, dated from about 250 BC, were discovered. Six of these can be seen at the County Museum

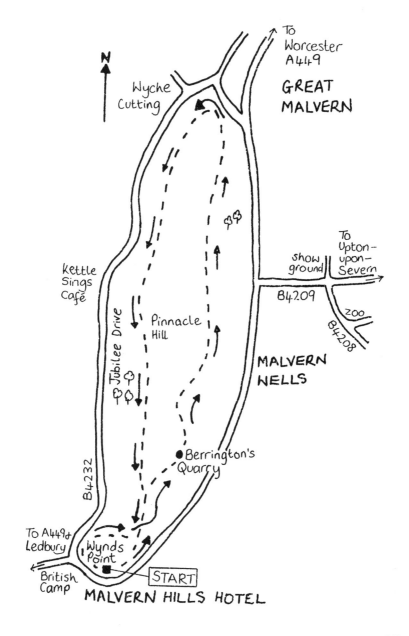

N

Wyche Cutting

To Worcester A449

GREAT MALVERN

Kettle Sings Café

showground

To Upton-upon-Severn

B4209

ZOO

B4208

Jubilee Drive

Pinnacle Hill

MALVERN WELLS

B4232

Berrington's Quarry

To A449 & Ledbury

Wynds Point

British Camp

START

MALVERN HILLS HOTEL

British Camp.

at Hartlebury. Gallows were perched above the Wyche Cutting in medieval times.

Having walked through the cutting, you will be on Walwyn Road. There are toilets and a tea shop here. Turn left, taking the Elgar Route along Jubilee Drive. On reaching a car park take the path on the left, at the Malvern Hills Conservators sign. You are now walking just above the road. The path begins to rise and, as it does so, the view extends over Herefordshire towards the Black Mountains in the distance. Many of the benches along this route are memorial seats. At the next junction of paths and seat, take the lower path, entering woodland and bracken.

As you reach the quarry opposite the Kettle Sings tea shop, walk across the car park and continue along the wide path, parallel with the road. You will now be able to see the British Camp ahead, slightly right. At the next fork and bench take the lower path. At the following junction bear left along the higher path. Join the main track and make your way back to the car park and path to the pub.

Places of interest nearby

Near to the Three Counties Showground, which is on the B4209 Upton upon Severn road, is a children's zoo and miniature railway. *Great Malvern* itself is a lovely town with many interesting buildings.

8 Upton upon Severn
The Kings Head

The Kings Head, situated close to the river Severn, is ideally placed for both river and road traffic. It stands almost next door to the Upton old church, now known as the Pepperpot or Bell Tower. A unique cupola, added by the architect Anthony Keck in 1770, makes this an outstanding building. A Water Festival takes place in August and, with events at other times of the year, makes this little town a veritable hive of industry and a delight to visitors.

The pub has a cosy bar with interesting old signs decorating the walls. An inn for over 250 years, it once provided stabling and accommodation for the horse-drawn traveller. A pleasant lunchtime or evening can be enjoyed in this delightful setting. Water traffic moves peacefully up and down the river while ducks and other waterfowl go purposefully about their business and the passenger boat fills with tourists anxious to explore the further reaches of the river Severn. There is a spacious lounge and dining area where children are very welcome. A functions room leads out onto a large patio overlooking the river and food is served there during the summer months. A warm welcome awaits those visiting the Kings Head, where you can not only partake of good home-cooked lunches and dinners but also enjoy a cup of tea or coffee and a toasted tea cake. The bar menu offers such starters as mushrooms stuffed with soft cheese and garlic or crispy coated Brie. Main meals include daily 'Specials' which could be a tasty chicken tikka masala or the more conventional, though just as delicious, chicken or beef pie. Salads and sandwiches or a filled jacket potato provide a lighter meal. The vegetarian is catered for with a choice of interesting dishes. A children's menu consists of the usual favourites and there is a traditional Sunday lunch. Puddings are a 'must' – the treacle sponge and apple and blackberry pancakes, for example, are quite delicious. This is a Whitbread house and the beers served include Flowers, Boddingtons and Tetley. Guinness and Murphy's are on offer for the devotees of stout, while Heineken and Stella are the popular lagers. Four guest rooms are also available. The pub is open 'all day' from Monday to Saturday in the summer, and from 10.30 am to 2 pm and 5.30 pm to 11 pm in the winter. The normal Sunday hours apply throughout the year.

Telephone: 01684 592621.

How to get there: Upton upon Severn lies just off the A4104 Pershore to Little Malvern road. Approaching from the north, cross the bridge over the river Severn and turn left into the town. Immediately past the Pepperpot with its distinctive cupola, turn left and you will see the pub on your left.

Parking: There is some parking space outside the pub. Upton has two other car parks, both well signed.

Length of the walk: 3 miles. Map: OS Landranger 150 Worcester, The Malverns and surrounding area (inn GR 853405).

A pleasant, easy walk, without hills. Footpaths and lanes of the town are used to begin the route, before entering open farmland leading to the river path through watermeadows for the return. Herons stand motionless in the shallows and the abundant river life makes an ever-changing scene as you wander along this well-walked path.

The Walk

Assuming that you have left your car at the pub, walk into High Street. Go over the crossroads and continue into Old Street straight ahead. Make for the church of St Peter and St Paul, locally called the new church. There is a car park opposite. Take the footpath to the left of the church. Before doing this, it is interesting to note the flood-mark low down on a pillar by the entrance to the church from the road.

Walk along the footpath to the T-junction and turn right. On reaching a road, turn left. Rectory Road will now be on your right. Keep straight on through a housing estate. Where the road turns left you will turn right along a drive, Laburnum Walk. This soon becomes a footpath. Keep on this path, crossing over a road. After passing a small cemetery on your right you will go into an estate of bungalows. Follow the road, curving left and then right and passing Old Hall on your left. Now cross, diagonally, the grassy area on your left or follow the path round it. Take the footpath, which goes between wire fences, until you reach Rectory Road. Turn left. Almost immediately, at the T-junction, turn right and curve left into a lane.

On reaching Buryend Farm, a black and white building on your left, carry straight on through the farm buildings. Continue until you reach a footpath sign in the right-hand hedge. Ignore the stile there and keep straight on, with the hedge on your right. Keep close to the hedge for the next 40 yards, to where you come to a gap and division of the hedge. There could be a pole fence here. Go through the gap, or over the fence, and into the next field, still keeping straight ahead but with the hedge now on your left.

Make for the stile ahead. Climb this into the next field, where you will see a wide ditch, usually dry. Keep left of this, along the line of trees, to a wide stile, ahead. Go over this and then walk diagonally across the field towards a stile in the right-hand corner. You are now at the river Severn, opposite Sandy Point. Do not go over the stile, but turn left along the river bank.

It is a pleasant stroll through the watermeadows back to Upton – a few easy stiles to cross and river life to watch. We saw herons and black-backed gulls here during an April walk. The Malvern Hills make a dramatic backcloth to the town and the Pepperpot a good landmark.

On reaching a River Authority notice and a seat on your right, you can choose your route back to the Kings Head.

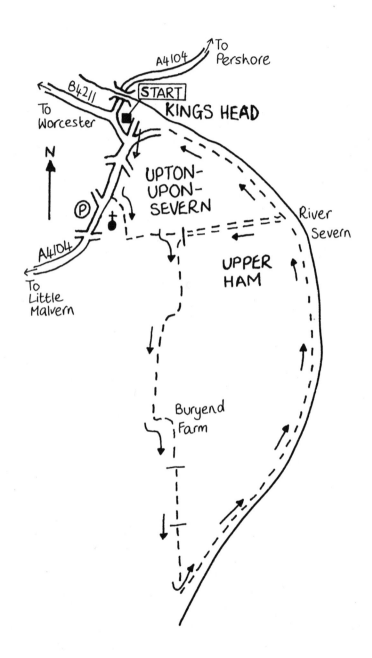

River Severn.

Option one is to turn left through the field along a wide track. You are in Upton Upper Ham, an area of Special Scientific Interest (Nature Conservancy Council). Pass through the gate, up the track and back into Laburnum Walk. Go straight ahead and retrace your steps to the car park or pub.

Option two is to continue along the river. This will bring you back into the town, passing the riverside buildings, into Dunns Lane and so back to the Kings Head.

Bredon
The Fox and Hounds

The history of Bredon can be traced to the hill of the same name and the fort built there during the second century BC. It is known that a church and monastery were destroyed here by marauding Danes in AD 850. The village, today, has in no way been spoilt by the close proximity of the M5 but features lovely black and white cottages with their flower-filled gardens and thatch.

This lovely inn with its 'eyebrow thatched' roof has been dispensing food and drink since the 16th century. Sympathetically extended during the last 50 years, the friendly, family run pub has retained much of its character. An inglenook fireplace, exposed timbers, beams and brasses make it a delightful place in which to enjoy the comfort and hospitality offered by the landlord and staff. Cotswold stone building materials and the flagstone floor came from an old barn which used to stand on Bredon Hill.

An extensive range of bar food is offered, while an à la carte menu is served in the more formal restaurant. The Sunday lunches are much in demand. The chef prides himself on providing a variety of dishes at all times, using fresh, local produce. Children are welcome in the spacious dining areas and a special menu for them includes whole baby fillet of plaice, a 4 oz rump steak, a small ploughman's lunch and an egg and cheese salad – grown-up sounding meals with children-sized portions. For the adults, the choice is almost unlimited. To mention but a few – giant New Zealand mussels baked with garlic and breadcrumbs, king prawns tossed in garlic butter, chicken samosa, lamb cutlets with mint sauce or a BIG mixed grill. Salads and soups, faggots and peas or steak and kidney pie are for the more traditional eater, while the daily blackboard offers a selection of sweets to tempt even the most serious dieter. The real ales are Boddingtons, Hook Norton and 6X. Heineken and Stella Artois are the popular lagers, with Bulmers Traditional and Red Rock draught ciders. An extensive wine list is available, but perhaps just a glass of chilled white is your preference? The Fox and Hounds is open from 11 am to 3 pm and 6 pm to 11 pm on Monday to Saturday, with the usual Sunday hours. Food is available whenever the pub is open, seven days a week.

Telephone: 01684 72377. 712311

How to get there: Bredon lies between the M5 (access from junction 9) and the A435 Evesham to Cheltenham road. From the A435 take the turning to Beckford, about 8 miles from Evesham, and continue through Kemerton. On reaching the village of Bredon go over the railway bridge and take the first turn right, signed 'Church and River'. The pub is on your right in about 200 yards.

Parking: There is plenty of parking space at the pub.

Length of the walk: 3³/₄ miles. Map: OS Landranger 150 Worcester, The Malverns and surrounding area (inn GR 920370).

This route takes in many aspects of country life. It starts in a lane alongside the river Avon, and continues on well-defined and signed field paths and tracks. Walk through the typical Worcestershire villages, with their thatched cottages and lovely gardens. If you look carefully from one enclosed path you will see a miniature train station

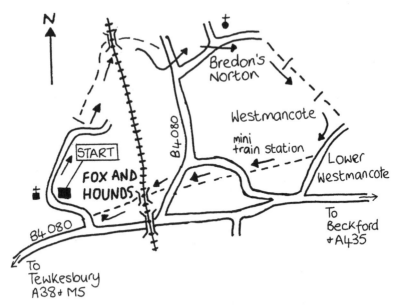

hiding among the bushes and trees which now encroach around it. Bredon Hill broods over this delightful area, protecting the villages from the worst of the weather and affording a recreational place for many people. There are no serious climbs.

The Walk

From the pub car park turn left, passing between the school and the car park. This soon becomes a narrow path. In high summer the gardens bordering the path are superb. Continue downhill until reaching a road. Turn right and walk along beside the river towards a boatyard. Bear right, uphill. On the brow of the hill there is a footpath sign, on your left, pointing down an enclosed path to 'Bredon's Norton ¾ mile'. Take this path, through the gate. Do not go down towards the river, but make for the next gate. Beyond this, the views are extensive across to the Malvern Hills, over the M5 and the railway line. The river Avon flows immediately below.

The next field was cropped when I walked through it but a metre width had been left through the centre. Make for a gap, ahead, with a waymark sign pointing to the right. At a gap, another waymark sign, turn right and pass under a tunnel. The main line railway passes overhead. Continue along this track until you reach a road, the busy B4080. Turn right for a few yards, then carefully cross over and take the minor road, almost opposite, signed 'Bredon's Norton'. This is a relatively quiet lane.

Walk uphill towards the village, about ¼ mile. Ignore the footpath sign on the right as you pass through the village but take the first lane on the right. The church is just off the road, here, on the left. Continue, slightly uphill, for about 100 yards. Look for a footpath sign in the hedge on your right. This is marked 'Westmancote 1 mile'. Climb the stile and walk across the field to the next stile almost opposite. Go over this and, keeping to the left of the field, walk down to the next stile, located in the hedge at the bottom left-hand corner. Cross this stile and the small bridge into the adjacent field.

Still keeping close to the hedge on the left, about 20 yards before reaching the bottom hedge, look for a gap. Go through this and turn left on entering the adjoining field. Make for a wide gap ahead and turn right along the track, with barns ahead. Continue along this track and go over a stile beside a riding school. Pass through the next gate onto a lane. Turn left. At the junction turn right.

You are now in Westmancote, a delightful village nestling at the foot of Bredon Hill. Walk, downhill, through the village until you reach a converted chapel on your right. There is a signpost here to 'Lower Westmancote'. Follow this and turn right along the top of the field, with a waymark just ahead. At a bend there is another waymark which points round the edge of the field. This is the right of way direction. However, when I was there the field was cropped and a metre width had been left through the centre, which was a much more convenient route as I was making for the gap opposite. Whichever way you go to reach it, walk through the gap onto a narrow, enclosed path through a wooded area. Here you have the surprise of a complete miniature train station, 'Frogfurlong Spa'. A waiting room, Hudson soap sign, even a wooden bridge over the lines, it is all there . . .

Continue along the path until reaching a road. Cross over and take the path signed 'Bredon'. Follow the tree line across the field until reaching another road. Cross over, carefully, and take the track opposite. Walk over the railway bridge and turn left along a wide, mown, grass track. Bear right at the bottom of the slope, with the

The river Avon at Bredon.

trees and stream on your left. Make for a stile. Go over this and turn left up a stony lane towards two stiles and a gate. Pass through the gate and turn right. Walk along the lane to the junction. Turn right to return to the Fox and Hounds.

Places of interest nearby

Bredon has an interesting old *tythe barn* which you may wish to visit. To do this, from the pub join the B4080 and turn right. In about 300 yards you will see a sign for the barn. It is in the care of the National Trust.

Tewkesbury is 4 miles away. Take the opportunity to visit this Gloucestershire town, with its beautiful abbey and maze of narrow alleys. Traditional shops still line the streets and the watermeadows of the 'Ham' lie between the rivers Severn and Avon.

⑩ Beckford
The Beckford Inn

This traditional inn dates back to the 1800s and has been refurbished without spoiling its charm and character. Set in 4 acres of gardens and greenery, with a patio furnished with seating for the warmer days, it also offers accommodation in en suite rooms. The comfortable interior is welcoming and friendly.

Steaks are a speciality, but there is much more on offer besides these. You could, perhaps, choose beef in Guinness pie or battered cod and chips. Haddock, plaice, scampi and prawns are also available as main courses. Children are welcome and can sit anywhere in the bar area. They can choose their food from the main menu and the prices are halved for them. The no smoking room is ideal for those who wish to keep their families away from the bars. Vegetarians are sympathetically catered for and salads are a speciality, with a generous mix of usual and unusual ingredients. Desserts are at one set price and include such temptations as treacle tart and apple pie. Sunday lunch is popular and booking is advisable. A local brew, Beckford Bitter, is a beer you may well like to try, or you could have a Theakston ale, a Guinness or a Murphy's stout. The opening times are 10 am to 2.30 pm and 6.30 pm to 11 pm, with the usual Sunday hours. Food is served from 12 noon to 2 pm and 7 pm to 9 pm. Telephone: 01386 881254.

How to get there: Beckford lies just off the A435 between Cheltenham and Evesham. The pub is beside the main road, at the T-junction giving access to Beckford village.

Parking: There is a large car park at the pub.

Length of the walk: 3½ miles. Map: OS Landranger 150 Worcester, The Malverns and surrounding area (inn GR 980352).

Wide tracks, easy stiles and waymarked paths all contribute to the pleasure of this scenic walk. While Beckford and Conderton are both, essentially, Worcestershire villages, they do have a Cotswold 'feel' about them. Stone cottages and a well-kept green in Beckford will encourage you to sit and let the world go by, as you appreciate the peace in this lovely place.

The Walk
From the pub car park turn right along the A435 after leaving the layby. Walk along the grass verge for about 20 yards, passing Bridge Cottage. Just past the cottage is a metal gate leading into a field. There is no footpath sign but it is a right of way. Go through the gate and cross the field, making for two stiles, close together and clearly visible. Go into the adjoining field. Walk, diagonally, passing between a dead tree and electricity pole, to the stile in the corner next to a cottage on your right. Go over the stile and into the lane. Turn right and pass the manor house. On reaching the crossroads, turn right. Cross over as you approach the church on your left and walk through the gate into the churchyard. Pass in front of the main doorway and bear to the right.

The lovely Norman church is situated next to the Hall. This once had a monastery based upon it. Now in private hands, it is not open to the public. Go through the kissing gate and into an enclosed pathway. The gardens of the Hall are on your right.

On reaching the lane turn right. Continue along the track as the lane ends, signposted 'Bredon Hill'. The hill rises to a height of over

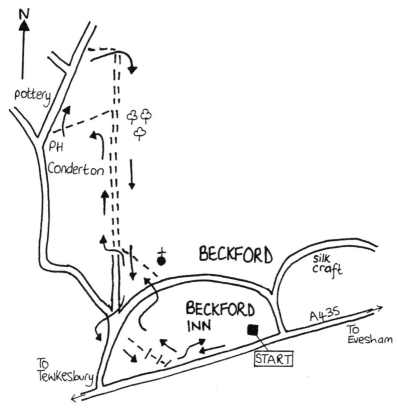

900 ft and this walk does not pursue the route to the top. However, follow the signpost for the time being. On reaching some farm buildings, bear left and then right, keeping to the track. You will now begin to walk uphill until you reach twin trees and a track on your right. Turn left at the yellow arrow sign, and keep on the path, with the hedge on your left. There are views here to the Malvern Hills. At the end of the field, go through the gate into the adjoining field. Ignore the gap and gate on your left and continue to a stile. Notice the manor house on your left. This is Conderton Manor. On reaching the lane turn right. This is where, by turning left, you can make a detour into Conderton itself – another pleasing, Cotswold-style village, with an interesting pottery and many attractive cottages.

Having turned right, or made your way back to this point, walk, quite steeply, uphill for about 500 yards. As the lane bends to the

Silk craft workshop, Beckford.

left walk straight on up a track. At a fork bear right and pick up a bridleway sign. This is a lovely part of the walk, with wide-reaching views taking in the Cotswolds, Dumbleton Hill and the Malverns. Broadway Tower can be seen in the distance.

At a junction of tracks, turn right, following the blue arrows. The walk now goes downhill, with panoramic views across the Vale of Evesham. You will recognise the twin trees ahead, where you join the original track. Keep on this back to the lane. Instead of going through the churchyard, continue straight ahead until reaching the crossroads. Notice the old milestone in the centre of the island. Retrace your steps along the lane, over the field and back to the pub.

Places of interest nearby

A *Silk Craft Centre* is just outside the village, where silk screening is carried out to patterns for the National Trust, Buckingham Palace and other major clients.

A pottery and silk designer are in the nearby village of *Conderton*.

11 Broadway
The Swan

Featured in so many tourist books and renowned as one of the prettiest villages in England, Broadway is also a mecca for walkers. The Cotswold Way passes through, while village paths and other rights of way circle like spokes of a wheel from the hub of this attractive place. Small arcades with a variety of specialist shops, antiques and fine arts for the connoisseur, books and fancy goods, the choice is yours. Many cafés and several pubs provide refreshment for visitors. The popular, busy Swan is situated in the main street.

There is a large, comfortable lounge and spacious dining room. Children are particularly welcome and have a special menu. All the usual favourites are included, with a few more unusual dishes such as lasagne with garlic bread or mini sausages with potato twisters. Banana and strawberry sundae or a profiterole with ice-cream and chocolate sauce make exciting sweets. For the adults, a comprehensive menu is complemented by a daily 'Blackboard Special'. A wide range of dishes are to be found, from cod and chips to chillies or salads. All are quickly served, in generous portions, by friendly staff. An outside seating area is available during the summer months, with gaily coloured umbrellas and an abundance of flowers. For cooler days, there is comfortable seating round a welcoming fire. Traditional beers include Whitbread real ale and a guest which changes monthly. Wines and ciders, lagers and spirits are served from the well-stocked bar. The Swan is open from 9.30 am to 11 pm (10.30 pm on Sundays). Food is always available.

Telephone: 01386 852278.

How to get there: Broadway lies on the A44, midway between Evesham and Moreton-in-Marsh.

Parking: There is limited parking at the pub, but a public car park just off the Snowshill Road, behind the church, is well signed.

Length of the walk: 3 miles. Map: OS Landranger 150 Worcester, The Malverns and surrounding area (inn GR 095375).

Lying beneath the northern escarpment of the Cotswolds, Broadway is on the edge of the Vale of Evesham. This walk takes in the climb up to the tower, with its views from 1,000 ft across the vale towards the Malvern Hills. The route, over easily followed paths and including part of the Cotswold Way, though necessarily uphill in places, has been chosen for its more gradual inclines. Take a look at the deer, donkeys, highland cattle and other animals as you enter the country park.

The Walk

From the pub turn left and walk up the main street of the village. As you almost reach the turn for Stratford-upon-Avon, Leamington Road, cross over and walk up a tarmac drive, signed 'Public Footpath'. At a fork keep to the right to a waymarked gate. Go through the gate and bear left along a pathway to another gate and stile. Over the stile, you pass through an avenue of trees known as 'The road to the woods'. Generations of farmworkers used this track up to the woods to collect wood for use during the winter.

Keeping the hedge on your right, walk straight uphill. There are views from here across the vale to Bredon Hill. Bear slightly

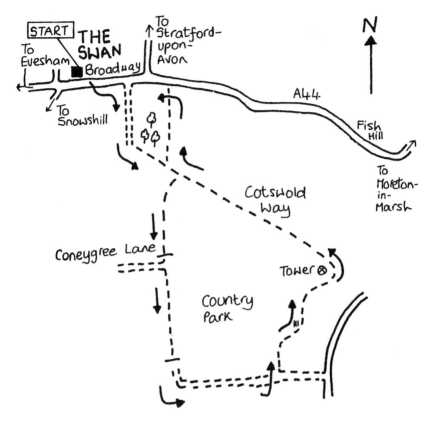

left towards a gap, waymarked. Make for the next gate on your right, again waymarked, and keep straight on to a stile. I heard a green woodpecker here one July evening. Cross the stile and go diagonally right to the waymark ahead. Now make for the next sign, visible ahead, noticing the spring and rushes on your left. Go over the stile.

The Cotswold Way goes straight on from here, following the line of the wall on your left. We leave it as a wide grassy track goes off to the right. This field, where there is evidence of quarrying, is known as Quarry Breche, obviously named from the operations, carried out on the hillside above, which have become grassed over. Much of the stone used for early building in Broadway was taken from here. Go through the next iron gate, which should be unlocked. There is another good view stop here. Keep straight on, following

Broadway Tower.

the old hedge line – a few shrubs and part-hedgerow still exist in places. Continue on the obvious path until reaching a gate and stile. Pass through this onto Coneygree Lane. This name comes from the rabbit breeding which took place here when the monks from Pershore Abbey were allowed to use it for that purpose. The name means 'rabbit wood'.

Continue straight ahead to the iron gate and stile. Go over the stile and make for the bungalow on a hillside to your left. Pass in front of the building, following a stone track. Turn left at the junction. Walk uphill now on the tarmac drive. Pass a farm and a cottage on your left. In about ¼ mile there is a gate and stile on your left. Go over this stile and make for the ladder stile diagonally right, close to the trees. Cross this and you are in Broadway Country Park territory. Walk to the left of the buildings, following the fence past the admission hut where there is a gate on your left which leads towards the tower.

A full history of the tower is available in the shop, while a plaque outside gives a summary. In 1800 the Earl of Coventry built the tower to please his Countess. It raised the height of the point to just over 1,000 ft and could be seen from their home in Pershore.

Pass behind the tower, go through a gate and turn left along the well-marked Cotswold Way. Follow this back to the village, entering the main street just east of the track you used when you began. Turn left to return to the Swan.

Places of interest nearby

Broadway Tower and *Country Park*, passed during the walk. Children will be delighted with the play area and adventure playground.

Snowshill Manor, a National Trust property, is signed from Broadway.

12 Honeybourne
The Thatched Tavern

Honeybourne consists of two villages, Cow Honeybourne and Church Honeybourne, both now being known as Honeybourne. However, locally, Cow Honeybourne is west of Icknield Street, the Roman road, and Church Honeybourne east. Both places had churches, and appear to do so even today. Not so. The church with the tower is now three houses, although the stranger would never know. The beautiful slender spire of the parish church is visible from most aspects of this walk. Honeybourne can be traced back to Anglo-Saxon times, when it was known as Huniburn – 'the stream, on the banks of which honey is gathered'. It has retained the sound, if not the spelling, of its original name.

The pub's name describes it very well. A listed building of the 16th century, it is one of the oldest buildings in the village. An 1851 census shows it as being licensed for the sale of beer and cider. The Tavern, as it is known locally, is a comfortable village inn. A spacious lounge bar, with a dining room leading from it, provides a friendly place to

exchange news and views for its many customers. There is an open fire in winter. Children are welcome and can be seated away from the bar area. The pleasant garden is suitable for them to play in during the warmer weather. Food is served in generous portions, and there is a variety to suit most tastes. A 'Specials' board tells of the dishes of the day, which vary according to season. Asparagus is a 'special' for about six weeks during the early summer. Served with brown bread and butter, it is a delicacy few can resist. Sandwiches, salads and jacket potatoes with a choice of fillings are always available. The vegetarian is catered for, as is the vegan with a 'Barnaby's Beanfeast'. Children are offered smaller portions at smaller prices. A freehouse, the Tavern serves real ales – Boddingtons Mild and Bitter, Theakston Old Peculier and Best Bitter. Strongbow and Gold Label are also popular drinks. Murphy's stout and Heineken lager are among other draught brews. The opening times are 11 am to 2.30 pm and 6 pm to 11 pm on weekdays, with the usual Sunday hours. There is no food on Tuesday evenings.
Telephone: 01386 835404.

How to get there: From Evesham take the turning off the bypass, to the east, signed 'Badsey'. Go through Badsey to Bretforton. After passing the Victoria pub on the B4035, take the second turning on the left, signed 'Honeybourne'. Drive along this road until you reach the village. The road bends left, with the church tower on the right, and the pub is just round the bend on the right.

Parking: There is a large car park at the pub.

Length of the walk: 2¹/₂ miles. Map: OS Landranger 150 Worcester, The Malverns and surrounding area (inn GR 116440).

This walk explores the field paths around the village of Honeybourne. A Vale of Evesham village, it is almost on the county boundary and has the distinction of having had two churches in different dioceses. You pass both on the walk. The way is well marked and has easy stiles.

The Walk
From the pub turn left and left again towards the 'church' (three houses). Turn left into the Leys, a recreation area. There is a

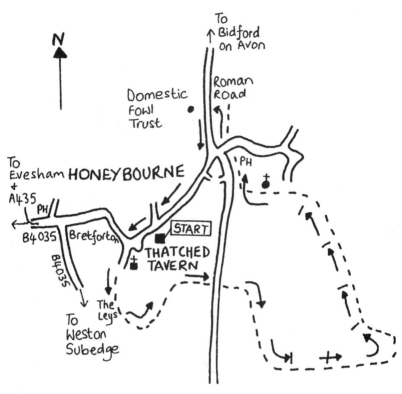

fingerpost pointing straight ahead. This is not the route you will take, so bear left across the football pitch to a point behind the goal post, where you will see a stile, waymarked with a yellow arrow. You will follow these yellow arrows most of the way.

Walk along the footpath until you see a sign on the left. This points two ways. Ignore the arrow to the left. The footpath actually goes through the middle of the field, but if it is cropped you will need to follow the hedge line. This means walking on for a few yards and, as the track carries straight on, turning right along the boundary. On reaching the end of the field turn right and walk straight ahead to a road, where there is a waymarked stile. Over this, cross the road carefully and go over the stile slightly to your left. You will now be able to see the church spire of Church Honeybourne on your left. Pass a red-brick house and continue along the well-defined path to a waymarked stile. Go over this, turn right and walk to the end of the

The church that isn't!

field, where you turn left, following the boundary hedge. The next stile is just slightly right as you reach the end of the field. Go over this stile and continue straight ahead. At the end of this field bear slightly right, then pass over two stiles and a wooden bridge over a ditch.

Continue straight ahead, with the hedge on your right. As the field ends, bear slightly right towards an electricity pole and a wooden bridge. Go over this and the stile. The footpath goes round this field to reach a stile which should be visible at the left corner. The yellow arrow should also be visible. Cross over the bridge and stiles and walk straight ahead towards the church and waymarked stile. Climb this and walk on towards a stile entering the churchyard. A barn and shed are on your left.

This is St Acgwin's church and is now the parish church for both parts of the village. If you would like to look inside the building you will need to apply to the vicar for the key.

Leave the churchyard by the path leading to the left of the main entrance door and continue to a waymarked gate. Go on along the tiled path until reaching a road. Turn right towards the Gate Inn and crossroads. You are now on Icknield Street, a Roman road.

To visit the Domestic Fowl Trust, keep on the same side of the road where there is a footpath. Go over the crossroads and walk for about 300 yards straight ahead. You will see the entrance on your left.

To return to the car park, make your way back to the crossroads, turn right and walk along the High Street. You will pass China Corner with houses named after famous potteries. I am told that a shop selling china once stood here, now a house known as The Thatches.

Place of interest nearby

The Domestic Fowl Trust cares for rare breeds from all over the world. Baby chicks are in a box in the entrance shop – children will love them. There are also swings and slides, books and souvenirs. Open daily (except Friday) throughout the year.

Evesham
The Navigation

The Navigation is first referred to in a vestry notice for a meeting at All Saints church, Evesham in 1807. Known as the Crown in those days, it, quite naturally, took its present name from the prosperous waterway which flows past its door. In 1840 the landlord, who was also in business as a coal merchant, had his own wharf on the bank of the river Avon, opposite. Nowadays, the Navigation has been brought up to date, with various improvements to its comfort. It still retains the air of a 'local', while also welcoming visitors.

The large garden area includes swings and slides for the youngsters, with seating and tables so that you can eat outdoors during the summer months. Indoors, a family room caters for the cooler days. The bar and lounge are comfortably furnished in a traditional manner. There is friendly and efficient service and the menu offers such popular fare as cod fillet and chips or lamb balti. A blackboard menu changes daily. Kid's Corner, as it is called, should keep the children happy, with dishes to suit them. The Navigation is a freehouse and serves M&B Brew XI and Mild. Bass and Guinness are also on draught. Ciders and lagers along with a selection of wines and spirits are all offered in this well-stocked bar. The opening times are 12 noon to 3 pm and 7 pm to 11 pm on weekdays, with the usual Sunday hours.

Telephone: 01386 446151.

How to get there: On approaching Evesham from any direction, follow the 'Town Centre' signs. When you reach the traffic lights south of Abbey Bridge over the river Avon, at the junction of the A44, turn eastwards on the B4035 to find the Navigation in Waterside, 200 yards along on the right.

Parking: There is a large car park at the pub.

Length of the walk: 2½ miles (without ferry 3½ miles). Map: OS Landranger 150 Worcester, The Malverns and surrounding area (inn GR 036432).

An interesting walk, through riverside meadows and over field paths. There is some road walking in the summer, and a little more in the winter when the ferry does not operate (open from April until October). Waterfowl compete with boating enthusiasts to gain space on this busy part of the river Avon. Fishermen sit, stoically watching their floats as walkers pass close to their boxes and bags of equipment.

The Walk

From the pub, turn left and walk towards the bridge. Cross over and turn right at the lights. A sign on your right points to the recreation field alongside the river. This area is pleasantly shady in summer. Walk left, following the river, until you reach a development of apartments. Turn left and keep to the tarmac path, uphill, towards the Bell Tower. Standing 110 ft high, this tower was built in 1539 and is part of a now ruined Benedictine abbey. Abbot Reginald's Gateway, a 12th century timber-framed building, leads from here into the market square. The battle of Evesham is well documented. The Almonry Museum, close by, which is now also the information centre, has this famous battle well illustrated. Local vale history is also represented. After going under the archway of the Bell Tower, walk straight ahead between the two churches. Bear left towards a gate leading onto a busy town centre road.

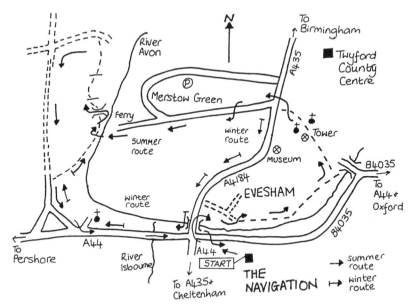

For the route which includes the ferry crossing (April to October), cross the road and turn slightly left onto Merstow Green. There is a large car park in the centre. Keep to the left of the car park and make for the road leading down to the river and ferry, which is signed. This road soon narrows to a lane, which terminates at the river bank and ferry. Cross the river by the ferry and turn right, following the footpath signs along the bank.

For the route which does not include the ferry (winter months), instead of crossing into Merstow Green, turn left after leaving the churchyard, passing the museum on your left. Continue to walk down the road towards the bridge. Cross over and turn right along the pavement towards Hampton. After passing the church on your right, ignore the immediate turn to the right and take the next one. In a few yards you will see a sign to 'Ferry and Town Centre'. Walk down this path to the ferry and turn left along the river.

There is a caravan/chalet park on your left. The wide, mown grass track continues straight on, following the river, but, for this walk, bear left after passing the last of the caravans, through a wide gap. Follow the path, diagonally right, uphill, through the field. The path gradually narrows until it reaches a stile, gate and

The ferry at Evesham.

bridge (waymarked). Climb the stile, cross the bridge and turn right towards another waymarked stile. Look back here for views across the town to the Cotswold hills. Keeping the hedge on your right, follow the well-defined path through the fields until you reach an orchard on your left and a planted garden on your right. Sewage works are also on your right.

At the cross-track, turn left along a wide, stony track. On reaching a junction of tracks, turn left. Follow this rather rough, wide track for about ½ mile, when you will reach a housing estate. Continue straight on to a fork and turn left, with a butcher's shop on your right, and reach the main road. Turn left. You are now in the Hampton district of Evesham. Continue to walk along the pavement, passing the church on your left, until you reach the bridge and so back to the pub.

Place of interest nearby

Twyford Country Centre, situated just off the A435 Evesham to Birmingham road, about 2 miles from the town. Children can hand-feed lambs and goats, and a falconry presents displays of its birds of prey.

14 Pershore
The Angel Inn

A delightful market town, Pershore has retained its charm, with many traditional shops still lining the streets. One of its oldest inns, the Angel sits conveniently opposite the Square. Built in the late 1600s, its age is reflected in its architecture. It is known to have been an inn since 1720. The furnishings are in keeping with, and the many beautiful arrangements of flowers set off, the dark wood and beamed ceilings. A garden leads down to the river Avon and is a delightful spot to hold summer barbecues. Accommodation is also available, in 16 comfortable en suite rooms.

Children are made welcome here with a suitable menu for them from which to choose their meal. The chef prides himself on the variety of food in both the bar and dining room. Local produce is used wherever possible as, in this market gardening area, fresh vegetables and salads are at their best. Filling snacks for a cold day are the home-made soup or a hot pork and stuffing bap, while a sandwich of smoked salmon and cucumber or deep fried lemon sole should suit those with an appetite for sea food. There is also a 'farmhouse breakfast', which is just what it sounds – ample helpings of bacon, sausage, eggs, mushrooms, tomatoes and fried bread. The vegetarians are not forgotten, broccoli and cream or potato and leek bake being but two dishes from the selection on offer. The puddings are mouth-watering. Treacle sponge and custard, lemon meringue and fresh cream or the ever popular apple pie are just a few. There is a Sunday lunch. Real ales are featured at the Angel. Castle Eden and Flowers Original are just two of them. The bar is open from 10 am to 3 pm and 7 pm to 11 pm on weekdays, with the usual Sunday hours.

Telephone: 01386 552046.

How to get there: Pershore lies on the A44, midway between Evesham and Worcester. The Angel is just north of the Square.

Parking: There is parking at the rear of the pub.

Length of the walk: 3¹/₂ miles. Map: OS Landranger 150 Worcester, The Malverns and surrounding area (inn GR 949458).

Pershore Abbey, the site of a major monastery in its day, dominates the town. This route takes you through some of the streets and pathways before a gentle walk along the river Avon. You will skirt Tiddesley Wood, where the first 'Pershore' plum tree was discovered in the mid 1800s. Views are spectacular from the ridge and the opportunity to visit the beautiful abbey should not be missed. The route is easy to follow and does not have any steep climbs.

The Walk

From the Angel turn left along the A44 towards Evesham. Cross the road and, as you approach the bridge, look for a tollhouse on your right. Take a few steps along the adjacent footpath (you are not walking that way) to see the crinkle-crankle wall.

Return to the road and continue towards the bridge. At the first stile on your right cross into the field and walk diagonally towards the river. Go over the stile and, keeping the river on your left, follow it for about 1 mile, crossing stiles and wooden bridges en route.

This is by no means a lonely stretch of river. Fishermen, boats and walkers are usually in evidence. After about ¹/₂ mile, do not take the path leading away towards a housing estate, but walk on

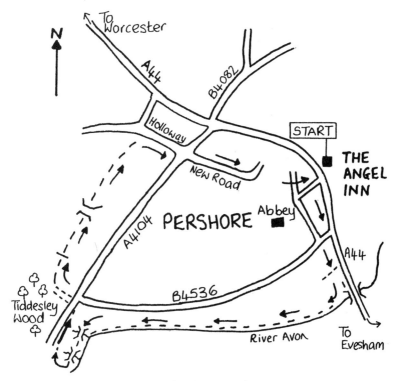

until you reach a set of two double stiles and bridges close together. After crossing the last of these, turn right through a field, keeping the hedge on the right. On reaching a catching-pen, climb the stile onto the main road, the A4104. This is a busy road and care should be taken as you cross it. There is a wide, mown grass verge to walk on as you turn right for about 200 yards. At a bridleway sign on your left and a tarmac drive, turn left. You will be rewarded as you reach the top of the drive by the sight of a lovely thatched cottage in front of you. Take the waymarked gate to the right of it.

Make for a stile in the right-hand corner of the field. Go over this into the next field, which you cross diagonally, towards the top left-hand corner and another stile. Cross this into an enclosed path, with a stream on your left. At least, there is supposed to be a stream but it might be dry. Go over a plank bridge and turn right until joining a track leading through cropped fields.

A bridge over the Severn near Pershore.

The trees on your left are Tiddesley Wood, cared for by the Worcestershire Nature Conservancy Trust. Do not turn left towards them, but take the marker sign pointing straight ahead. You will now cross a ridge with views for miles. Bredon Hill towers above and Pershore Abbey is below. At the road turn right. This is known as the Holloway. Walk, downhill, to the main road. Turn right, cross over, carefully, and take the road almost immediately opposite, New Road.

Continue down this road until reaching a junction, with a factory shop on your right. Walk straight ahead, leaving the road, with railings on your right. A car repair workshop is on your left. The abbey looms ahead. Follow the footpath round and then straight ahead, emerging next to a school. Cross over and take the paved path towards the abbey, passing between the bowling green and abbey grounds. You now have the opportunity to visit the abbey, where there are explanatory booklets to help you enjoy this lovely place. Leave the grounds by the gate to your right and walk into the Square.

Place of interest nearby

Pershore Horticultural College is just outside the town. This is open on many days throughout the summer.

⑮ Spetchley
The Berkeley Knot Inn

This inn takes its name from the Berkeley family who owned and lived in the nearby Spetchley Park. The present house was built in 1810 with a massive Ionic portico. A story of war and destruction lies behind the pastoral beauty of today's parkland. Used by Cromwell's men as a garrison during the Civil War, it was recaptured by the royalists, who had no choice but to burn down the original house, being unable to afford to defend it.

The landlord has old photographs of the Berkeley Knot, taken in the early 1930s, when it was a petrol filling station as well as an inn. Sympathetically modernised in later years, this friendly pub is comfortably furnished in a traditional manner. Spacious rooms and well-served meals justify its enviable reputation for the service it provides. There is a pleasant garden for summertime eating and relaxing. Children are welcome and there are various dishes to suit them. The main menu is varied and includes such meals as ham off the bone or a home-made steak and kidney pie. Rump or sirloin steak with a variety of vegetables is another popular choice. Sandwiches, salads, jacket potatoes and ploughman's lunches are all served in generous portions. A choice of four vegetarian meals is also offered. For the thirsty, the real ales in this freehouse include Pedigree, Hook Norton and M&B Mild and Brew XI. Four lagers are on draught. The malt whiskies, wines and spirits available should please most tastes. The opening times are from 11 am to 3 pm and 6 pm to 11 pm on Monday to Saturday, with the normal Sunday hours.

Telephone: 01905 345293.

How to get there: Spetchley lies east of Worcester on the A422 (from Worcester follow the signs for Evesham and Stratford-upon-Avon). Just east of Spetchley Gardens take the B4084, signed 'Evesham' and 'Pershore'. The Berkeley Knot is about ¼ mile along this road, on the left.

Parking: There is a large car park at the pub.

Length of the walk: 2½ miles. Map: OS Landranger 150 Worcester, The Malverns and surrounding area (inn GR 910535).

This route, on well-marked paths, takes in some fine views of Spetchley Park and grounds. I saw a herd of deer in the parkland and Canada geese closer to the house. There is some road walking but on an adjoining footpath. The stiles are good, there is a railway bridge to cross and the changing scenery from parkland to cropped fields makes this an interesting and satisfying walk.

The Walk

From the pub car park turn right. Walk past a row of houses and cross the road, carefully, to a footpath sign opposite. Go through the gate and proceed along a wide track to a stile ahead. Enter an enclosed path and go over the next stile and onto a track. As the track bends, go straight on towards a bridge over the railway (main line). There are wooden steps – be careful in wet weather.

Take the track ahead, following the right-hand hedge line. At the end of the track, turn right through a gap and, almost immediately, go over the stile on your left. If the next field is cropped, there is a metre path left through it. If not, then walk straight ahead towards a stile. Go over this into the parkland of Spetchley Park. Continue straight ahead, keeping left of a wooded area. As you approach the

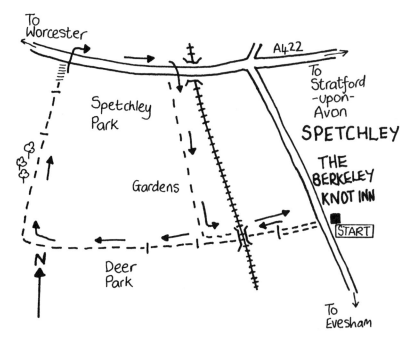

house you will see a lake on your right and a ha-ha wall. Go over the stile close to the wall. This is where you will probably see the geese. Continue through the adjacent field, which, if cropped, should have a metre path, to the next stile into parkland again.

Here you will see another elevation of the house with its impressive Ionic portico. The deer park lies to your left. Climb the next, visible, stile. Ignore the stile on your left and continue straight ahead, following the fence closely and walking towards a small wood. On reaching the wood, turn right. Ignore the stile which leads into it and follow the fence alongside the trees. Continue until you reach a catching pen and a gate. Go through the gate, then walk diagonally, slightly right, passing between a single oak tree and the fence until reaching a hedge where you will see a stile. Go over this and another one, down to the main A422 road. Be careful to control children here as it is tempting to run down the steps straight onto the busy road. Cross over, carefully, and turn right. Walk under an attractive metal bridge and on to the entrance into Spetchley Gardens.

Spetchley House.

Continue along the main road for about another 300 yards until you see a bridleway sign on the opposite side of the road. Cross over, carefully, go through the gate beside the sign and walk along a rather rough track. In about ¼ mile, look for a stile on your right. Do not go over it. You climbed this one earlier in the walk. Go through the gap on your left and walk on the path, keeping the hedge on your left. Make your way towards the railway bridge which you crossed before and follow the outward route back to the pub.

Places of interest nearby

Spetchley Gardens are open to the public during the summer, except Saturdays. There is a small shop and tearoom here.

You may like to pay a visit to the *Countryside Centre*, which is about 2 miles from the pub on the Worcester road (well signed).

16 Hanbury
The Country Girl

This is a comfortable, rural, 150 year old pub. It has been comprehensively refurbished but retains much of its old world charm. Original oak beams and reclaimed bricks make a perfect setting for the many antique farm implements and tools which decorate the walls and it is good to see that the original fireplace has been retained. A pleasant no-smoking area has been created from two derelict cottages adjacent to the pub. They have been converted into an attractive conservatory which has vastly increased the lounge area.

Children are very welcome and there is plenty of space for them, both indoors and outside. Junior sized meals are prepared and priced accordingly. A feature of the Country Girl is its incredibly varied menu. Meals are displayed on a blackboard and change from day to day. Examples of possible dishes are curried prawns and pineapple, smoked haddock with orange and rosemary, vegetable lasagne, or lamb with apricots and walnuts. Lunchtime quick snacks may include jacket potatoes, sandwiches, ploughman's lunches and a tasty soup.

Many different beers are stocked. Marston's Pedigree, Boddingtons, Wadworth 6X and Flowers Original are the real ales. The pub is open from 11 am to 3 pm and 7 pm to 11 pm on weekdays, with the usual Sunday hours. Food is served from 12 noon to 2 pm and 7 pm to 9 pm (Tuesday to Sunday).

Telephone: 01527 821790.

How to get there: The pub is situated on the B4091 between Hanbury and Stoke Prior, east of Droitwich and the M5. From Droitwich, pass under the M5 and join the B4090. Continue on this road until you reach Gallows Green. Take the next left turn, which leads you past the Hanbury Hall entrance. At the T-junction, turn left and continue on the B4091 for about 2 miles, until you see the Country Girl on your left.

Parking: There is a large car park at the pub.

Length of the walk: 4 miles. Map: OS Landranger 150 Worcester, The Malverns and surrounding area (inn GR 957657).

A walk which includes a variety of terrain – a short, steep climb, woodland tracks, open fields and the opportunity to visit the lovely National Trust property of Hanbury Hall. The Jinney Ring Craft Centre is also passed on this walk, with its fascinating collection of craft shops arranged in an old barn conversion. Hanbury church, of 'The Archers' fame, is another interesting point of call.

The Walk

Leave the pub car park from the back entrance and turn left down the lane. Turn left at the first fork. Pass between some houses and, as the tarmac road ends, walk straight ahead towards the wood. Bear slightly right and join a cinder path leading into the woodland. Keep on this path, ignoring left-hand forks, and you will, in about ¾ mile, reach a track. Turn right and then bear to the left. There are waymark signs from here. Pass a farmhouse on your right and continue ahead over a stile into a field. The path bends to the left as it reaches a hedge. Climb the stile and follow the path, uphill, towards the church which can now be clearly seen.

Go through the gate into the churchyard. Keep to the right of the building, through the gate and down the lane. Pass two houses on

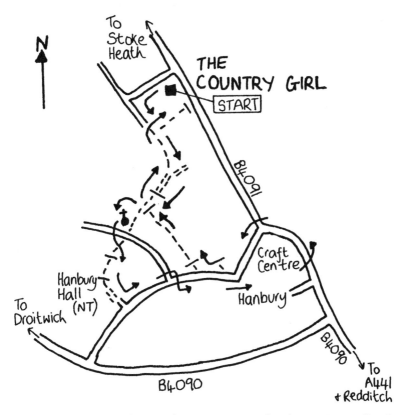

your right. Bear right at the junction and, almost immediately, look for a National Trust sign and waymark on your left. Go through the gate and cross the field towards the next, clearly visible, stile. Continue to follow the path towards the drive into Hanbury Hall.

On reaching the drive, turn left and go left again at the lane. Continue until you reach a fork to the left leading up to the school and church. Do not go up this lane but look for a footpath sign on your right, almost opposite the turn. There is a parking layby and the path crosses a stile behind it. Go over the stile and follow the field paths towards the Jinney Ring Craft Centre, which can be clearly seen on the left. Enter the centre close to the duck pond.

The Jinney Ring Craft Centre, Hanbury.

Leave the Jinney Ring by the main entrance and turn left, then left again. Walk along this lane until you see a footpath sign on your right. Pass this and walk on to the next sign. Climb the stile here and this is where you have the steep, short climb – up to the church. If you want to avoid this, then walk on past the footpath sign until you reach the lane leading past the school to the church. This is still rather steep, but is comfortable to walk.

The footpath enters the churchyard by an iron gate to your left. Leave by the gate at which you entered on your outward route. Now follow the paths back through the woodland to the end of the cinder track. Cross the lawned area and join the lane. Almost immediately, look for a stile on your right. Go over this and, keeping the hedge on your right, bear right towards a wooden gate. Go through this onto the road and turn left. You will see the pub ahead.

Places of interest nearby

The National Trust property of *Hanbury Hall*, the *Jinney Ring Craft Centre* and *Hanbury church* are all included in the walk. Hanbury Hall is open from April to the end of October, on Saturdays, Sundays and Mondays (2 pm to 6 pm).

17 Stoke Prior
The Ewe and Lamb

It was in 1922 that John Corbett, who became known as the 'Salt King', finally effected the transfer of the salt works from Droitwich to Stoke Prior. The source of supply was much nearer to Stoke than to Droitwich and he hoped to gain a mineral of greater quality by so doing. Many changes have taken place since those days but it was the work of Corbett that was partially responsible for salt becoming a cheap everyday commodity, instead of the luxury item it previously was. The village, consequently, ceased to be rural and became an important industrial site. However, today, while relatively close to Bromsgrove and other major towns, it is still possible to walk the tracks and pathways around this erstwhile small settlement.

The Ewe and Lamb is conveniently situated for such a walk and offers a children's 'paradise', with all kinds of their favourite activities, from bouncy castles to balloons, face painting and the like, during the summer months. There are swings and slides and an outdoor play area where adults can sit comfortably to watch the games. Spacious, both inside and out, this pub offers a friendly atmosphere and a good selection of both food and drink. The menu is geared to cater for all ages. Grills, salads, soups and a variety of children's dishes are attractively presented and quickly served. A Whitbread house, four real ales are available – Boddingtons Bitter, Flowers IPA and Original, and Wadworth 6X. There is a choice of three lagers and the usual wine and spirit list. The opening hours are from 11 am to 11 pm on Monday to Saturday throughout the year. On Sundays the pub is open from 12 noon to 3 pm and 7 pm to 10.30 pm. Food is available every day from 11.30 am to 10 pm.

Telephone: 01527 871929.

How to get there: Stoke Prior lies just south of the A38 between Bromsgrove and Droitwich. The pub is on the B4091, about 500 yards south of its junction with the A38 at Stoke Heath.

Parking: There is ample parking at the pub.

Length of the walk: 2^1/$_2$ miles (3 miles if you include the extension to the Avoncroft Museum of Buildings). Maps: OS Landranger 150 Worcester, The Malverns and surrounding area contains most of the walk, but Landranger 139 Birmingham and surrounding area has the starting point (inn GR 925788).

This interesting route can incorporate a visit to the Avoncroft Museum of Buildings. You start on an old track leading over the river Salwarpe and then walk beside the Worcester and Birmingham Canal to Bayers Warehouse, returning to the pub along a quiet lane. With easy to follow paths and no hills, this is a walk for everyone – and for all seasons.

The Walk

From the Ewe and Lamb cross the road, with care, to the signed, tarmac bridleway opposite. Continue straight ahead along this track, which soon becomes a stony path. Looking to your left as you walk, you will be able to see the windmill in the grounds of the Avoncroft Museum and, to the right, the steeple of St Michael's church. Cross the bridge over the river Salwarpe and walk up the drive, between some pretty houses, onto Fish House Lane. There is a bridleway sign here. Turn right and right again when you reach a kissing gate set in a brick wall, at a footpath sign.

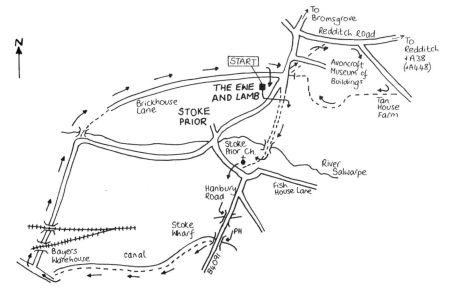

Continue along this path until you reach the churchyard. Enter through the waymarked gate and make for the church entrance. Take the pathway leading straight on (the designated footpath) and cross Hanbury Road, carefully. Turn left and walk along the pavement, passing Fish House Lane on your left. Continue along this road, using the wide pavement for about ½ mile, until you reach the Navigation Inn at Stoke Wharf. You will need to cross the road here as the pavement finishes when it approaches the bridge.

Go over the bridge, turn left down the canal steps and turn left again to go under the bridge. There are numerous buildings alongside the wharf and longboats tied up here. This peaceful stretch of canal takes on a rural atmosphere as it leaves the warehouses behind. Only the radio masts tower ahead. The towpath is not a right of way, but walkers are allowed to use it. In about ¼ mile you will pass over a humped bridge just before Bayers Warehouse appears on the opposite side of the canal.

Leave the canal at the next pathway, which will bring you out opposite Stoke Prior Sports and Country Club. Turn right along Westonhall Lane to the junction with Shaw Lane. Turn right. Pass under two railway bridges and continue straight ahead on the wide pavement. When the road bears sharply right, take the path going

81

Avoncroft museum.

straight on, signed 'footpath', and cross the river Salwarpe again by a wooden bridge. Follow the footpath round to a metalled track, along a gently rising incline. The lane widens and passes a farm and some houses. This is Brickhouse Lane, an access road with very little traffic. Proceed along this leafy, pleasant lane until you reach the Ewe and Lamb on your right.

To incorporate the Avoncroft Museum in your walk, continue past the pub and cross the Hanbury road again. Take the footpath sign immediately opposite, directing you through a gate into a park, with the cricket field on your left. Go through the next waymarked gate onto a tarmac drive which leads to the college and art school. Cross over this drive, go through another gate and make for the gate in the right-hand corner. This will bring you out onto the main Redditch to Worcester road. You can walk the 200 yards or so on the grass verge or cross over onto the pavement opposite. Take the first turn right, signed to the museum, and enter through the gate on the right.

You can either walk back the same way or take a field path which is slightly longer but includes some interesting features. Leave the museum through the same gate by which you entered and turn right along Buntsford Hill. In about 250 yards you will reach West Croft and Tan House Farm. Turn right here, at the footpath sign. Pass through the farmyard, keeping straight ahead to an iron gate. Go through this, keeping to the right. Ignore the metal gate on your left. Keep the hedge on your left and walk straight ahead to a stile. Cross this and walk diagonally left to the next visible sign. The windmill in the museum grounds will be on your right as you join an enclosed path following the edge of the grounds. You will pass a wild flower conservation meadow on your right as you walk along. The path turns sharp right. Continue to follow the wire fence and bear left to the waymark sign ahead. Cross the field diagonally towards the footpath sign and the main road, where you will see the pub opposite.

Place of interest nearby

The Avoncroft Museum of Buildings shows a range of structures, from pre-fabs to a smock windmill. Farmyard geese, ducks and sheep wander at will through this interesting and well-planned site.

18 Lickey
The Poacher's Pocket

By no means a quiet country inn, this pub reflects the lively area in which it is situated. Close to the conurbation of Birmingham and district, it is also adjacent to the Lickey Hills Country Park. Walkers and family groups as well as passing motorists are made to feel welcome and comfortable here. This is a pub with a difference. One does not often find a theme portrayed so aptly and thoroughly.

But what is in the poacher's pocket? A 'Beater's' sirloin steak, perhaps, or a 'Bailiff's' big gammon steak. 'Tasty tickled trout' or a 'Stalker's' steak and kidney pie? To cater for the 'Young Poacher' the menu offers most of the children's favourites, followed by a free ice-cream. 'Secret Sweets' and 'Naughty Puddings' are a real temptation, and the Sunday lunch is very popular. Hot chocolate, ground coffee or tea are always available. There is a selection of real ales and traditional beers, Banks's Bitter and Marston's Pedigree, for example, to complement your meal. The opening times are 11 am to 11 pm on weekdays, with the usual Sunday hours. Food is always available.

Telephone: 0121 453 2795.

How to get there: Lickey lies between the M5 and the M42, north-east of Bromsgrove. From the junction of the A38 with the M42 (junction 1), take the sign for 'Lickey'. Pass the entrance to the visitor centre on your right and continue down the hill to the roundabout. The pub is just in front of you.

Parking: There is ample parking space at the pub.

Length of the walk: 3 miles. Map: OS Landranger 139 Birmingham and surrounding area (inn GR 000760).

The 524 acres of the Lickey Hills support a wide range of habitats for all types of flora and fauna. During this walk you will have the opportunity to witness many aspects of this delightful part of Worcestershire. A viewpoint with a toposcope, a monument to the Earl of Plymouth and the facilities offered by the visitor centre are all included.

The Walk

From the pub car park cross, carefully, over the busy road. Keep on the right-hand side of the road as you walk towards Rose Hill. Turn right, up the hill. Ignore the first footpath sign, which is almost immediately on your right, and continue up to the bridleway sign, about 200 yards away, on your right. Turn right along the track. The footpath goes directly ahead to the edge of the golf course, where it turns left to follow the course perimeter. However, it seems to be permissible to walk diagonally across the green towards the car park of the Rose and Crown. On reaching the car park, keep to the fence behind it. Follow the cinder track to a gate on your left. Go through this, with the golf shop on your left. Now take a stony track alongside the bowling green and join the North Worcestershire Path. Go up the steps ahead. Turn right and follow the 'North Worcestershire Path' signs. This path follows the golf course perimeter. Leave it as you reach the bottom of Beacon Hill, where you will see the toposcope on your left.

Edward George Junior and Henry Cadbury gave Beacon Hill to the city of Birmingham in 1907 for leisure and recreation. The toposcope, which looks rather like a fortress, was restored in 1987/8

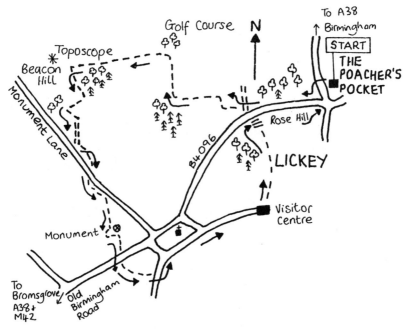

as a Manpower Services project with support from the Cadbury family. The toposcope was originally built purely for the far-reaching views that can be enjoyed from this hill.

Turn away from the toposcope towards the car park and walk diagonally left in the direction of the pine woods. Take the path at the edge of the trees, where you should be able to see Bittell lakes ahead. At a cross-tracks keep straight on, downhill. On reaching some shallow wooden-edged steps and a bench, turn right along a track, ignoring a flight of steps on your right. Join a wide cinder path and walk towards a fence leading onto a lane. Do not go on the lane but turn left and follow the woodland path until you reach the end of the wood and a garden wall. Join the lane here and cross over. Turn left.

Continue walking along this pleasant tree-lined road until you reach a waterworks site. Just round the bend you will see an entrance into an area of rhododendrons and other shrubs. As you walk into this well-kept lawned enclosure you will see the impressive monument to the 6th Earl of Plymouth. It was erected in his memory by the Worcestershire Regiment of Yeomen Cavalry. Walk round

Toposcope, Lickey.

the monument to the memorial plaque and make for the group of trees, where there is a clearly visible footpath. As you emerge from the wood onto the main road, cross over, carefully, to the garage opposite. Turn left.

In a few yards you will see a path leading through the cemetery. Walk along this to the lychgate at the other end. Turn left along the road towards the church. At the fork take the right turn, with the church on your left. You will now join the entrance track to the visitor centre, used by vehicles as well as walkers.

Leave the centre by rejoining the track. Turn right and make for the upper car park. Just as you enter the car park, turn left along the path marked 'Bilberry Hill'. Pass between pine trees. At a fork bear right and join a gravel path. Turn left and progress along this woodland path to where you will come to a viewpoint on your left. Continue along the path, ignoring a right fork, until you reach a flight of wooden-edged steps. Walk down these to the gate at road level. You are now back at Rose Hill, where you turn right and make your way to the pub.

⑲ Wolverley
The Queen's Head Inn

Wolverley's old centre, of church, school and aged red-brick houses, is situated on a red sandstone escarpment above the Stour valley. Steep roads have been cut through the sandstone to connect the village with the church and, in the other direction, with the village of Cookley. Within these red sandstone cliffs, caves have been cut. As you drive your car into the large car park to the left of the pub you will be directly under a sandstone outcrop with a row of these caves. Wide entrance apertures, overhung with elder bushes, make a sharp contrast to the deep red stone.

This pub has a long history. In 1861 the beer brewed here was known to be the second strongest in England. With a gravity of 1060, it was brewed to an old Black Country recipe – in those days there were no cars and no breathalysers. A story of a white swan and a broken wedding ring is a local legend. I am sure someone in the bar will be willing to relate it to you ... The lounge area in the Queen's Head is warmly welcoming, with comfortable furniture. Children under 14 are asked to use the family room, which leads out behind it and is suitably furnished and equipped. There is a garden for your use during the summer. A good pint is served in this Banks's pub. Camerons strong bitter is a very popular brew. Draught Strongbow cider and draught Guinness also have their following. The usual lagers are available, as are a range of wines and spirits. The 'Pint and Platter' menu offers more than the normal bar snacks. There is always a home-made special of the day, but who could go wrong with Whopper Cod or a Yorkshire Bucket (beef and four vegetables served in a Yorkshire pudding)? The delicious ploughman's, too, is all a ploughman's should be, and vegetarians are not forgotten. The youngsters will enjoy the food from their own menu, which offers a choice to please most small appetites. Sponge puddings and custard or fruit salad and ice-cream are among the sweets served here. The opening hours are 11.30 am to 2.30 pm and 5.30 pm to 11 pm on weekdays, with 'all day' opening (11 am to 11 pm) on Saturdays and bank holidays. The usual Sunday times apply.

Telephone: 01562 850433.

How to get there: Wolverley lies about 1 mile north of Kidderminster. From the A442, turn northwards onto the B4190 and continue on this road until the B4189 crosses it. Turn right for a few yards and then left. This road leads into Wolverley. Follow signs for the village. The Queen's Head is on your left, just over a bridge.

Parking: There is ample parking at the pub.

Length of the walk: 2½ miles. Map: OS Landranger 138 Kidderminster and Wyre Forest area (inn GR 830793).

A walk of mixed terrain – field paths, cuttings through red sandstone and a lovely canal towpath. Take a look at the old Wolverley 'Pound', cut out of sandstone, where stray animals were once impounded. Pretty cottages, bedecked with flowers in the summer, and a cheery call from the holidaymakers aboard the canal boats make this well-marked route a delightful relaxation.

The Walk

Leave the pub and turn left, up the hill through the Holloway. Notice the building on your right. This was a grammar school, opened in

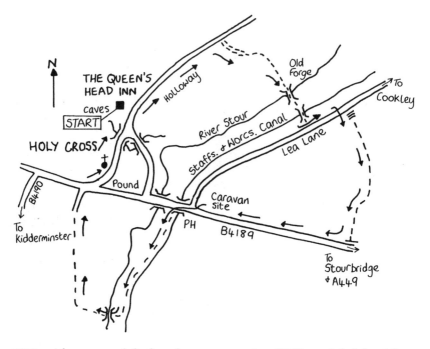

1720 with money left for that purpose by William Sebright. The school became a public school in 1948 and closed in 1970 after 250 years. The Holloway is aptly named, being literally a hollow way cut through the sandstone rock.

At the top of the hill, pass Drakelow Lane on the left and walk on for about 100 yards, until you reach a lane leading off on the right. Turn into this, known as Shortyard, and pass some cottages. The lane becomes narrower and reaches a field. Ignore the footpath sign on your left to Blackeshall Lane.

As soon as you enter the field, turn right and follow the easily defined path through it, downhill, towards the Gloucester Coppice. Climb the stile as you emerge from the coppice, cross the field towards the bridge and pass over another stile. Cross the river Stour by the stone bridge and note the old mill leat. There was a small and very early industrial settlement here, of which the mill was part. Pass Forge Cottage, go over the canal bridge and turn left into Lea Lane. Cross the road and take care round the bend.

Sandstone caves near Wolverley.

You will see a flight of stone steps and a footpath sign on your right. Climb the steps into the wood and follow the path until you reach a fence of larch lap fencing. Turn left, keeping close to the fence. At the end of the fence turn right onto a path running between some houses and a field. Ignore the 'walker' sign going off to the left and follow the metal footpath sign, keeping straight along the path. This may be slightly overgrown, but is passable with ease. The path ends in some steps down to the Stourbridge to Bewdley Road. Turn right. There is a wide footpath here. Keep on it, downhill, passing a caravan park on your right. On reaching the Lock Inn, cross the canal and turn onto the towpath. This is not a legal right of way, but walkers are allowed. There is a 'walker' sign, but it points the wrong way for this route. Instead, go under the bridge and take the path going towards Kidderminster.

This is an attractive spot and is particularly interesting on summer days as the pleasure boats line up to go through the lock. They are often bedecked with flowers or colourful decorations. Continue walking for about 300 yards along the canal bank. It was here that I saw a heron, poised on the edge of the bank, ready to swoop when he saw a meal flashing by. His sudden, startled, flight as I approached caused a great stir in the hedges as the smaller birds all took flight too. Sandstone rock on the other side of the canal, topped with wooded slopes, make this shady and lovely part of the walk a real delight.

On reaching a marker sign, turn right and cross an iron bridge over the river Stour. Walk through a watermeadow on a wide, easily followed path. This leads into a lane, passing Mill Cottage. Follow the lane round to the right into an estate of houses and join the Bewdley road. Turn right and walk towards the roundabout. Cross the road – the best place is by the school. You may like to walk down a few steps to see the old Wolverley Pound, carved from sandstone. This is a busy road and care should be taken when crossing. Now, take the lane almost opposite the school. This passes the church of St John the Baptist, which you may well wish to visit.

Continue down the winding hill, between a sandstone wall on one side and some delightful cottages on the other. At the bottom of the hill you will reach the pub and your car.

Places of interest nearby

Kinver, a few miles north of Wolverley, is an interesting place, with its many sandstone caves.

Kidderminster is the station from which to travel on the Severn Valley Steam Railway to Bridgnorth.

⓴ Holy Cross
The Bell and Cross

Holy Cross and Clent are about ½ mile apart and lie on either side of the A491 Stourbridge to M5 road, which carries the traffic away from the villages over a bridge. The Bell and Cross once stood in the centre of the shopping area. However, times have changed and now only the post office remains. The Clent Hills and a country park lie to the north-east and provide a relaxation area for people living in the adjacent large towns. The well-marked tracks and paths make for easy walking.

The taproom of the inn was a butcher's shop at one time and has the iron hooks of that trade still hanging from the ceiling. A deed of sale dated 1831 shows that the pub was in existence then and must have been trading as such long before that date. Its age is reflected in the beams and blackened oak furniture worn smooth with usage. The bar boasts an open fire to cheer a chilly day, while the old Smoke Room has been renamed the Garden Room, appropriately so, as it looks directly over a well-kept lawn and flower beds, which are a riot of colour in the summer. Tables and chairs with bright umbrellas make this a pleasant place to relax on warm days. The pub is a welcoming, comfortable one for all seasons, with friendly staff and quick service. A 10 oz gammon steak or a 12 oz rump should suit those with a hearty appetite. Jacket potatoes with a variety of fillings or soup of the day with a crusty roll make good snacks. The children's meals include most of their favourites, while a daily blackboard offers the 'specials'. The Bell and Cross is a freehouse serving a range of well-kept ales, including Banks's traditional Mild and Bitter and Marston's Pedigree. Harp lager, Bulmer's ciders and a range of wines and spirits are also offered. The opening times are 11.30 am to 2.30 pm and 6 pm to 11 pm on Monday to Saturday, with the usual Sunday hours. There is no food on Sunday or Monday evenings.

Telephone: 01562 730319.

How to get there: From the A456 Kidderminster to Birmingham road, turn off at Blakedown and make for Belbroughton. Go through the village, following signs for Clent. You will arrive at Holy Cross, with the pub on your right.

Parking: The pub does not have a car park. There is, however, room to park down the lane beside it.

Length of the walk: 3½ miles. Map: OS Landranger 139 Birmingham and surrounding area (inn GR 924788).

A walk on the Clent Hills. There are a few steep climbs, but plenty of seats from which to enjoy the views across to the Malverns and Abberley Hill. Enjoy the 'Sound of Music' feel as you emerge from the woods into an open field, with inspiring glimpses of distant horizons.

The Walk

From the pub cross the road and walk along Church Avenue, signed 'Clent'. Pass under the A491 road bridge and continue until you reach the church of St Leonard. There are some interesting houses here, one of which was the village school. Turn right at the church and proceed along the lane, passing Clent Hall on your left. In about ¼ mile, look for a white gate on your left and go through this into the field. Follow the path, diagonally, across to a metal gate in the right-hand hedge. Go through this onto a lane. Cross over and go through the gate

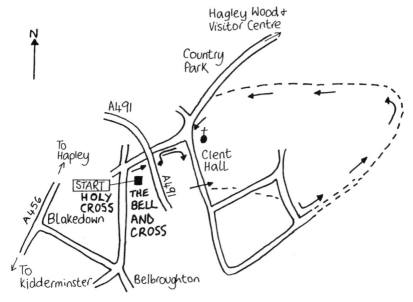

almost immediately opposite. Now walk, uphill, diagonally right, towards a duckpond and the hamlet of Walton Pool. Go through a gate onto a road. Turn right. You will see an old sign of the Cyclists' Touring Club on the wall of a cottage on your right.

Take the next left turn, into Highfield Lane, which soon becomes a path/bridleway. Climb up a single, stony track between fields, leading to the top of Walton Hill. Take a path skirting to the right, then the next indicated bridlepath to the left, to the top of Walton Hill and the trig point, which shows a height of 1,035 ft. There are many benches here from which to enjoy the views.

From the trig point take a left-hand path in a south-westerly direction, with the Malverns and Abberley Hill in the distance, leaving the Birmingham conurbation behind you. The path then passes down through woodland. Ignoring the first bridlepath on the right, take the next right-hand fork down through the trees to cross a stile into an open field with superb views.

Follow the path through the hedge line. Walk diagonally and fairly steeply across the next field to a stile. The path then skirts St Leonard's churchyard and returns to the lane and Church Avenue.

Severn Valley Railway.

Places of interest nearby

Kidderminster is close by, where you may like to either visit the station or ride on one of the trains of the *Severn Valley Steam Railway*. This line operates between Kidderminster and Bridgnorth in Shropshire, but there are stations en route if you do not wish to do the whole journey. An experience to savour as you step back in time to the days of steam and travel along the lovely vale of the river Severn.

The country parks of Clent/Hagley Wood are good places to explore. These open spaces and wooded areas have good parking places and information boards and are easily reached from both Clent and Holy Cross.